FREDERICK DENISON MAURICE

FREDERICK DENISON
MAURICE

BY

H. G. WOOD

CAMBRIDGE
AT THE UNIVERSITY PRESS

1950

PUBLISHED BY
THE SYNDICS OF THE CAMBRIDGE UNIVERSITY PRESS

London Office: Bentley House, N.W.
American Branch: New York

Agents for Canada, India, and Pakistan: Macmillan

Printed in Great Britain at the University Press, Cambridge
(Brooke Crutchley, University Printer)

CONTENTS

PREFACE

In his charming history of the House of Macmillan, Mr Charles Morgan describes F. D. Maurice as one of the Macmillans' closest friends and most prolific authors. The Macmillan brothers, Alexander and Daniel, regarded Maurice as a prophet. Mr Charles Morgan finds their enthusiasm a little puzzling. 'Though it may seem almost an insult on Alexander's memory to say so (for Alexander had no doubt of "the Prophet's" greatness), to a later generation of readers the Rev. F. D. Maurice himself will have to be a little explained.' If such explanation be indeed necessary, I hope the studies that follow will contribute to it, if only by encouraging some abler theologian to better them. But in any case I am persuaded that the present generation would gain from a closer acquaintance with the thought of Frederick Denison Maurice.

If I were writing a dedication for this volume, I should name first the Principal and Staff of Mansfield College, Oxford, who did me the honour of inviting me to deliver Dale lectures in the academic year 1942-3. I am further indebted to them for accepting my proposal to lecture on the place of Maurice in the religious thought of the Victorian Era. In a dedication I should wish to associate with the authorities of Mansfield College, the Faculty of Arts, the Senate and the Council of the University of Birmingham who appointed me first Professor of Theology in the University, and thus enabled me to enjoy six years of teaching when I could devote my chief attention to the theme of this book.

PREFACE

My debt to my predecessors in this particular field will be obvious, and is even greater than appears. I cannot, however, close this preface without two particular acknowledgments. I was encouraged to think my choice of subject not inappropriate for a lectureship founded in memory of a great Congregational divine, when the Rev. K. L. Parry drew my attention to Dr Mackennal's appreciation of the influence of Maurice on Congregationalists. Subsequently the Regius Professor of History in Oxford, Sir Maurice Powicke, lent me a copy of the *Congregational Quarterly* containing the striking tribute to Maurice by his father, Dr F. J. Powicke. In preparing the lectures to appear in book form, I have been able to draw on this admirable article. To the Rev. K. L. Parry and to Professor Powicke I tender my sincere thanks.

CHAPTER I

INTRODUCTION

I T may be desirable at the outset to offer some reasons for
devoting a series of Dale lectures to the teaching of
Frederick Denison Maurice. Dr Mackennal, in his book
The Evolution of Congregationalism, published in 1901,
suggested that 'the time has not yet come to estimate the
effect of Maurice on the religious and social thinking of
the century'. He added, 'I often suspect that when it
can be appraised, it will be seen that his abiding influence
has been, not on English Churchmen but on English
Congregationalists'.[1]

If confirmation and illustration of the truth of Dr
Mackennal's judgment be needed, it may be found in the
fine appreciation of the influence of Maurice which
Dr F. J. Powicke contributed to the *Congregational Quarterly*
in April 1930. His interest was first aroused by hearing
John Hunter preach in the Old Meeting House (the
Baxter Church) at Kidderminster. The teachings of
Maurice were mediated to Congregationalists by John
Hunter and J. Baldwin Brown and many lesser lights.
Dr Powicke became an ardent Mauriceian while a student
at Spring Hill. 'When I left Spring Hill, in the summer of
1877, Maurice meant far more to me than Simon [the
Principal] and this relation was never quite reversed,
though the latter's merits as a great teacher . . . gave him
an unique place in my affectionate reverence. I may be

[1] Op. cit., p. 206.

wrong, but I incline to think that a majority of our younger ministers in 1877 bore the Mauriceian stamp.' This might suffice to show that an estimate of Maurice should be of interest to Congregationalists, but since Dr Mackennal wrote, we have had several appreciations of Maurice and it might fairly be argued that any further estimate is superfluous.[1] Since 1901, we have had C. F. G. Masterman's sketch of his life and position as a leader of the Church. King's College, London, has made the *amende honorable* for depriving Maurice of his chair in 1853, by establishing a lectureship in his memory. Two series of these lectures have been published, one by Dr Scott Lidgett and the other by Dr Claude Jenkins, the first estimating Maurice's contribution to the Victorian transformation of theology, while the second appraised him not only as theologian but as educator and social reformer. Dr Raven has given us a sympathetic study of Maurice in his account of the Christian Socialist movement in this country. Still more recently an American scholar, Mr C. R. Sanders, in his book *Coleridge and the Broad Church Movement*, devotes the last third of the work to a full and judicious survey of the leading principles of Maurice, whom he regards as the main channel through which the influence of Coleridge was brought to bear on theology and philosophy in England. Where so much has been written already, further discussion may seem to be a work of supererogation. Yet perhaps something remains to be said. Mr Sanders prefaces his account of Maurice with the assertion that 'his figure seems to have lost some of its luster and strength in our day', and if this is the case, it may need more than one essay in appreciation to restore to his figure

[1] For a survey of recent studies of Maurice's teaching, see A. R. Vidler, *The Orb and the Cross*, p. 85.

the lustre and strength that clearly belong to it. I may note that if Maurice escaped debunking at the hands of Lytton Strachey in *Eminent Victorians*, he also missed inclusion among the portraits of *Great Victorians*, which the Massinghams edited, though it is true that his name is in the list of candidates whose claims were considered. Even now he is probably not estimated at his true worth, and he deserves a higher place in the ranks of the Victorians than he has yet received.

I shall be studying his life and thought in relation to the religious and social movements of his time, and I shall try to estimate afresh his significance for his own age. But my chief reason for choosing my present theme is not that there is still room for a further considered estimate of the influence of Maurice on the religious and social thinking of the nineteenth century. My justification must be found in my conviction that his legacy has not yet been fully appropriated and that his principles are peculiarly relevant to our own age. He was, I think, in advance of his time. His name is often associated with the Broad Church, and Mr Sanders who follows this tradition could appeal for support to the authority of Dr Fairbairn, who, in *Christ in Modern Theology*, associated Maurice with Thomas Arnold and Dean Stanley as leaders of the Broad Church school. Maurice had much in common with Arnold and Stanley, and enjoyed a close friendship with the latter. Yet, as Dr Scott Lidgett observes, he does not belong to any one school of thought. The impossibility of classifying Maurice may be due to his distinctive individuality. J. B. Mozley, who found him antipathetic and irritating, once wrote, 'As for F. Maurice, it is really no use to take him in hand. He is Mr F. Maurice, an individual, and that is all.' Dr Fairbairn suggested that

Maurice lived in a world of philosophical ideas, peculiarly his own. 'The theology of Maurice had its basis in philosophy and he read Scripture and history and institutions in the light of illuminating philosophical ideas.'[1] Certainly his approach was his own, and the special characteristics of his mind rendered his teaching unacceptable and indeed unintelligible to many of his contemporaries. But the real reason why we cannot classify Maurice is not so much the strength of his individuality, as the genuineness of his catholicity. It may be possible to-day to appreciate Maurice as never before. At a time when the Churches are drawing and being drawn closer to one another, we may well find illumination in his understanding of the nature of the Catholic Church. At a time when planning, national and international, is alike a fashion and a necessity, we may well return to the founder of Christian Socialism to learn the art of co-operation. At a time of renewed concern for Christian education, we may well examine afresh the principles and methods of one of the finest educators of the nineteenth century.

Mr Sanders offers three reasons for what he regards as a decline of interest in Maurice, and an examination of these reasons may introduce a closer study of his character and outlook. Mr Sanders says, 'That this figure seems to have lost some of its luster and strength in our day may be due partly to the changes in systems of values and modes of thinking which have taken place between his day and ours, partly to the vigorous exercise of mind that is required to understand and digest his thought, and partly to a method of self-effacement which he habitually employed in all that he said or did.' With regard to the first

[1] *Christ in Modern Theology*, p. 178.

reason, I am inclined to think that Maurice was more at variance with the systems of values and modes of thinking that prevailed in his own day than he is with those that prevail in ours. Many of the changes which have taken place between his day and ours favour a fuller appreciation of his position. The form in which he presented his teaching may be more distasteful to us than to his contemporaries. No man was more prodigal than he in publishing sermons, and the Victorians seem to have read sermons with an avidity which is sadly lacking in their degenerate posterity. Both the demand for and the supply of printed sermons have fallen off since the Victorians passed from the stage. Volume after volume of Maurice's works consists of sermons, and for that reason alone they often remain unread. But the content, if we digested it, would be found again and again to chime in with and anticipate many of our systems of values and modes of thinking.

The necessity of a vigorous exercise of mind to understand and digest his thought remains unaltered. Many of his contemporaries who were quite capable of such exercise of mind declined to make the effort. They formed the impression that Maurice was confused, inconclusive and ineffectual. We may recall Matthew Arnold's saying that Maurice was constantly beating the bush with great fervour without ever starting the hare. When his *Theological Essays* appeared in 1853, they made an unfavourable impression on James Martineau at first reading. He wrote to R. H. Hutton, 'I am reading Maurice's "Theological Essays" and find them notwithstanding a good deal of interest in parts, on the whole shadowy and unimpressive. I hardly think a man has any business to write till he has brought his thoughts into distincter shapes and better defined relations than I find in Maurice. He seems to me to have a mere presentiment of thinking, a tentative process in that direction that never fairly succeeds in getting home. But I have thus far read only some half-dozen of the essays.' J. B. Mozley, in writing to R. W. Church, was even more slashing in his criticism: 'I do not envy you your task of reviewing Maurice's *Theological Essays* in the *Guardian*. . . . It is a pity to see a man losing himself and becoming a ruin from a radical mistake of thinking himself a philosopher. Some of the cut-up reviews did much good in this way. They put down a man at the outset. But Maurice has been petted and told he is a philosopher till he naturally thinks he is one. And he has not a clear idea in his head. It is a reputation that the instant it is touched must go like a card-house.' This adverse verdict might be due to the fact that Maurice had suffered what the late Viscount Halifax regarded as the greatest possible misfortune that could happen to any man. He had been educated at Cambridge. Though he subsequently had the good fortune to become an undergraduate at Oxford and take his degree there, Oxford could not efface the formative influence of the sister university. His was still a Cambridge mind. Church, who had a great admiration for Maurice, felt that he was never at home in Oxford. In writing to Acton, Church says, 'He [Maurice] always seemed to me to lose his temper when talking of Oxford and the Oxford men.' So Mozley's critical attitude and rather contemptuous judgment are readily intelligible. But this cannot be the whole truth of the matter. Though Maurice exerted a great influence in Cambridge, perhaps a deeper influence before he became Knightbridge Professor of Moral Philosophy than during the brief years of his Professorship, yet

6

typical Cambridge men reacted to his teaching very much
in the same way as Martineau and J. B. Mozley. As
representatives of the Cambridge mind, few men can
compare with Henry Sidgwick and Leslie Stephen. Sidgwick felt that Maurice was an adept in looking difficulties
boldly in the face and passing on. He gives this enter-
taining picture of Maurice's method: 'In Maurice's hands
you feel like a horse being led up to a five-barred gate,
which is your theological problem. How will you get
over it? Maurice shows you the gate, dilates upon its
bars, its height, its insuperability, strokes your nose a
little more, and all of a sudden you find yourself looking
at the gate from the other side. You know that you
have not got over it legitimately, but how you find
yourself on the other side you do not know.'

Leslie Stephen was as severe as J. B. Mozley. In 1874 he
wrote an article on Maurice's Theology for the *Fortnightly*,
of which John Morley was then editor. In a private letter
he says, 'I am writing on Maurice for Morley. Of all the
muddleheaded intricate futile persons I ever studied, he
was about the most utterly bewildering. But I hope to
explain his vagaries tolerably.' His more considered
judgment may be found at the close of his article on
Maurice in the *Dictionary of National Biography*—the article
which Raven thinks Stephen should never have written.
There, with some insight, he attributes the muddle-
headedness which he detects in Maurice to 'his catholic
interest in all religious beliefs . . . and his excessive intellectual ingenuity in reconciling apparent contradictions.
The effort to avoid a harsh dogmatic outline gives an
indistinctness to his style if not to his thought and explains
why some people held him, as he says himself, to be a
muddy mystic.'

J. S. Mill, who had a very high opinion of Maurice's intellectual gifts—he reckoned him decidedly superior to Coleridge in merely intellectual power, apart from poetic genius—always thought that there was more intellectual power wasted in Maurice than in any other of his contemporaries. All these verdicts point to real weaknesses in Maurice as writer and thinker, but they underline the necessity of a vigorous exercise of mind if we are to do justice to his thought. If Maurice had really been a futile, muddleheaded person without a clear idea in his head, he could never have exerted the influence on Hort which we know he did. If Maurice had done nothing more than help to form the mind of Hort, he would be entitled to our respect as a thinker and teacher.

An early judgment of R. W. Church is also illuminating. 'There is something in Maurice and his master Coleridge, which awakens thought in me more than any other writings almost: with all their imputed mysticism they seem to me to say plain things as often as most people.'[1] Even more striking are Martineau's second thoughts. After alluding to the religious realism which was the distinction of the genius of Coleridge and which developed itself in the school of F. D. Maurice, he says of the latter, 'for consistency and completeness of thought and precision in the use of language it would be difficult to find his superior among living theologians'. Martineau made the effort to understand Maurice and found the effort to be worth while. In the light of his tribute we may discern the inadequacy and impatience of the estimates of J. B. Mozley and Leslie Stephen. We may also suspect that we shall not appreciate Maurice ourselves without being willing to make a strenuous exercise of the mind.

[1] *Life and Letters*, p. 17.

That in his own life-time and since, Maurice was and has been depreciated because of the demands he makes for mental effort is no doubt true. How far the lustre and strength of his figure have been dimmed by his method of self-effacement is more difficult to say. That he was almost morbidly self-depreciatory is true enough. He could not have been and he was not unaware of his real powers, and he was most anxious that they should not be overrated either by himself or by others. He was eager to acknowledge his debts, spiritual and intellectual. He believed he was entrusted with a message which he was unworthy to deliver, with a truth he was unworthy to declare. Like John the Baptist, if he had been asked whether he was a prophet he would have replied, No, a voice. He felt on occasion that particular messages were given to him. He wrote to his mother in 1837, 'I sometimes do find that words are put into my mouth which I hardly knew the meaning of before, and which seem to be spoken through me for the sake of those to whom God would do good. And though it humbles me to perceive how little I have to do with what I have thought and said and even that I have done what in me lay to cross the intention of God, yet it rejoices me to have this new proof of His graciousness and goodwill.'[1] His expressions of self-distrust and even self-condemnation were so frequent as to awaken in some minds the suspicion of insincerity. But the true nature of his self-distrust has been rightly interpreted by R. H. Hutton. It sprang from his reverence for Christ and from the tenderness of his moral sympathies. As R. H. Hutton says, 'the more Maurice believed in Christ, the less he confounded himself with the object of his belief and the more pathetic was his

[1] *Life*, i, 218.

9

distrust of his own power to see aright or to say aright what he saw'.[1] And to quote Hutton again, 'the tenderness of his moral sympathies gave him a double ground for self-reproach and self-abasement. He thought himself guilty of the guilt into the depths of which he had pierced, and he thought himself equally guilty of not having entered into its pangs more generously and with more healing power.'[2] Another aspect of Maurice's self-effacement, or rather of his never completely successful struggle to efface himself, is brought out in a discerning observation of Dr Dale. In the days of his retirement, Dr Dale wrote to a friend:

I am reading Maurice's life again. . . . He seems to have had more than a suspicion that the discomfort with which he received the affection and honour of his friends lay very near the root of all false relations to God. He did not quite learn the secret, but he nearly learnt it. What he wanted was to be conscious that he *deserved* all the love and trust that came to him. I am more and more clear about this, that we must be content to know that the best things come to us from man and God without our deserving them. We are under grace, not under law. Nor until we have beaten down our pride and self-assertion so as to be able to take everything from earth and heaven just as a child takes everything without raising the question, Do I deserve this or that? or rather with the habitual conviction that we deserve nothing and are content that it should be so, do we get into right relations with our Father in heaven or with the brothers and sisters about us. . . . The craving to *deserve* can never be satisfied: we have rather to try to be grateful for what we do not deserve.[3]

[1] *Modern Guides of English Thought in Matters of Faith*, p. 318.
[2] Ibid., p. 320.
[3] Dale, *Life*, p. 541. This passage from Dr Dale's life is worth recalling for its own sake. Even if Maurice was more successful than Dale supposed, how hard it is for the best of men to surrender the thought of making them-

Dale is certainly justified, if Maurice's constant self-depreciation is evidence of self-effacement not fully achieved. I have been led on to describe at some length this characteristic of Maurice, because it is an essential feature of the saintliness which so impressed those who knew him best and which makes a closer acquaintance with him a source of inspiration to us who come after. But whatever be the nature of the limitation of Maurice's habitual self-effacement, I doubt whether this has dimmed the lustre of his figure for our generation, though we may find that owing to his self-effacement, we are often Mauriceians without knowing it. For his own generation, his self-effacement never meant that he hid his light under a bushel. He did not do so precisely because he believed the light was not his. He was essentially the soul of chivalry, and he rushed to the defence of beleaguered truth like some intellectual Galahad. He was almost hypersensitive to misunderstanding and misrepresentation, not so much of himself, though he was as sensitive as Newman of any criticism which touched his honour and the honour of his profession. But his concern was for truth, and he flung himself into controversy after

selves worthy of God's grace. In one sense it is a laudable ambition, and yet how easily it becomes a retrogressive influence! Even T. T. Lynch's noble hymn, 'Dismiss me not thy service, Lord,' stands in need of revision, though heaven protect us from those officious editors who print hymns with the ominous letters 'alt.' in brackets at the foot of the last verse! But listen to this:

> Our Master all the work hath done,
>   He asks of us to-day,
> Sharing his service every one
>   Share too his sonship may,
> Lord I would serve and be a son,
>   Dismiss me not I pray.

Dale and Maurice would unite in reversing the order of service and sonship: 'Sharing his sonship every one/share too his service may,/Lord, I would be a son and serve,/make me a son, I pray!'

controversy. And in his case, controversy did throw light on the mystery of Godliness!

In the next chapter I propose to deal with Maurice's main principles as he set them forth in the Kingdom of Christ. I shall also describe the way in which he came to his principles. In the remainder of this chapter, I wish to remind you of the transformations which took place in theology in the Victorian era and to indicate in general outline the relation of Maurice to them.

Changes and developments in Christian thought come about either through fresh vivid apprehensions of some truth of the Gospel or through advances in knowledge, changes in the intellectual climate or through changes in the social-economic basis of society which may or may not find expression in events which compel attention and challenge thought. That these factors interact is certain, yet each must be regarded as an independent factor. The influence of social-economic conditions and of social-economic change may be more continuous and more pervasive than changes in religious outlook or scientific knowledge, but it is clear that the process of social-economic change itself is not a self-contained, self-determined process. It is influenced by religious and scientific factors as surely as these factors in turn are influenced by the social-economic environment.

We may start then from those apprehensions of the truth of the Gospel which were destined to change the current theology. When the convictions were forming in the mind of Maurice which led him to take orders in the Church of England in 1834, Calvinism was still the dominant strain in British theology. Indeed, in some quarters, among the Baptists for example, it continued to be so for a generation at least. When my father was a

student at Regent's Park in the 1860's, Dr Angus could
say to his students, 'Gentlemen, if you won't have
Calvinism, the Churches won't have you.' To-day it is
questionable whether the most worthy of Baptist deacons
is familiar with the five points of Calvinism or could
expound the scheme of salvation which every preacher was
expected to outline and enforce in every sermon. As we
look back, certain main features of Calvinist theology
stand out in high relief. The stress fell on the thought of
God, as Sovereign, Lawgiver and Judge. One might
almost say that God as Saviour was subordinate to God as
King and the Gospel subsidiary to Law. For the mercy of
God revealed in the Gospel was just this, that through
the substitutionary sufferings of Christ on the cross, God
was able to pardon the sinner while vindicating His out-
raged majesty and maintaining the requirements and one
might almost say the prestige of Law. But the doctrine
of election and reprobation meant that the benefits of
God's mercy accrued only to the elect few, and the
majority of mankind seemed to be destined to endure
eternal torment in hell.

It was at this point that the Wesleys and their followers
challenged the dominant orthodoxy. That Christ died
not only *for* us but *instead of* us, they were fully convinced,
and the wondrous love of His atoning death is the burden
of their preaching and the constant theme of their praise.
So far as the substitutionary view of His Atonement is
concerned there is no real difference between Toplady
and Charles Wesley, between 'Rock of Ages' and 'Jesus
lover of my soul.' But the Wesleys were sure that Christ
had died for all men, and that God had not ordained any
one for eternal torment. Let me recall one magnificent
expression of this hope of a universal redemption.

Father, whose everlasting Love
    Thy only Son for sinners gave;
Whose grace to all did freely move,
    And sent him down this world to save;

Help us thy mercy to extol,
    Immense, unfathom'd, unconfined;
To praise the Lamb who died for all,
    The general Saviour of mankind.

Thy undistinguishing regard
    Was cast on Adam's fallen race;
For all thou hast in Christ prepared
    Sufficient, sovereign, saving grace.

The world he suffer'd to redeem:
    For all he hath thro' atonement made:
For those that will not come to him,
    The ransom of his life was paid.

Why then, thou universal Love,
    Should any of thy grace despair?
To all, to all, thy bowels move,
    But straiten'd in our own we are.

Arise, O God, maintain thy cause!
    The fullness of the Gentiles, call;
Lift up the standard of thy cross,
    And all shall own thou diedst for all.

It is noteworthy that the Evangelical Revival initiated by the Wesleys dwelt so much on the pleasantness of religion and the goodness of God, and made so little use of hell-fire. The doctrine of eternal punishment in hell was not denied. In the *Hymns for the people called Methodists*, there is indeed a subsection describing Hell, but it contains only one hymn, and that does not describe hell, it insists on the desirability and possibility of escaping it! The traditional doctrine of eternal punishment was already in the 1830's arousing grave disquietude in the Christian mind. Such disquietude was destined to grow, and Maurice himself was destined to bring this disquietude to a head. But it is safe to say that increasingly throughout the nineteenth century men maintained the doctrine because they believed it to be strictly scriptural or because they regarded it as an integral part of the teaching of the Catholic Church, and not because they wholeheartedly believed it.

A belief of this kind is a belief accepted on authority, whether on the authority of the record of scripture or of the witness of the Church. In the 1830's the notion of revelation as the communication of truth in propositions on divine authority still dominated the Christian consciousness. The Evangelical movement did nothing to shake or refashion this conception. The divine authority was conceived to be found in a verbally inspired and inerrant Bible or an interpretation of such a Bible by a Church which was endowed with infallible authority in matters of faith and morals. The challenge to these conceptions of revealed truth and religious authority did not come exclusively or mainly from a deeper apprehension of the Christian religion, though these conceptions were already being transformed by the teaching both of Coleridge and of Thomas Erskine of Linlathen. But the effective challenge, particularly to the claims made for Scripture and Church, came from advances in literary and historical criticism, and in natural science. It is unnecessary to outline these advances which shook men's confidence in the historical and scientific accuracy of Scripture and of Church pronouncements at a time when such accuracy was assumed to be essential to their spiritual authority. Critical history had taken a decisive step with Niebuhr's work on the history of Rome, and it was no longer possible to deny the presence of myth and legend in the historic traditions of the Jews as well as in those of other peoples. The difficulties of harmonising Genesis with geology were only lost sight of in the greater difficulties of reconciling Moses with Darwin. Dr Rendel Harris was fond of observing that in theology it is a mistake to be born before Darwin! It was even more unfortunate that so many of Darwin's theological contemporaries were unable to assimilate the truth of his theory. Maurice had reached a position where he could defend freedom of enquiry in the study of both history and nature and where he could welcome the results of such enquiry. His example encouraged others to welcome new truth unafraid. On this side, as well as on the side of their social teaching and activity, Maurice paved the way for the Lux Mundi school. But I doubt whether he contributed much to the discussion of the issues raised either by the higher criticism or by the theory of evolution. He was not, in the ordinary sense, a critic. He was not, like some of the authors of *Essays and Reviews*, bent on smashing windows to let some fresh air into the stuffy edifice of orthodoxy. He deprecated and deplored the publication of Colenso's exposure of the arithmetical weaknesses of the Pentateuch. Maurice is conservative in his exposition of Scripture, and as Fairbairn said, he handled the Scriptures in the light of his philosophical principles, rather than in accord with the rising school of historical and literary criticism. Somewhat similarly, while he welcomed Darwin, he had not the interests which would qualify him to discuss effectively the relations of religion with the new trend of natural science. Unlike Kingsley he was no naturalist. He says of himself as a child that in the once familiar children's story, *Eyes and No-Eyes*, he resembled No-Eyes. Perhaps this meant that he did not realise the full gravity of the issues which frightened so many of his contemporaries. But he could face new discoveries with equanimity because his faith rested on another foundation than the traditional authority of Church or Bible.

Maurice was more fully alive to the wider movements of thought which marked the first half of the nineteenth century—the ethics and economics of the philosophical radicals and the positivism of Auguste Comte. While the latter arises from reflection on the natural sciences, the former were more closely concerned with the forces of political and industrial revolution. Utilitarianism in ethics erected 'the greatest happiness of the greatest number' into the standard of statesmanship. The philosophic radicals claimed for economics, recognition as a valid independent scientific discipline. Positivism claimed for the methods of the natural sciences a monopoly of all attainable knowledge. Maurice was concerned far more with Bentham and J. S. Mill than with Strauss and Renan, and far more with Comte than with Darwin. And as I shall seek to show, part of his real contribution to the religious and social thought of England is that he met the challenge of Utilitarianism and Positivism when these schools of thought were at the height of their influence.

Behind these changes in the cultural outlook were the far-reaching social changes due to the agrarian and industrial revolutions. The segregation of the classes in the big cities, the separation and conflict of class-interests in capitalist industry, the widespread poverty and degradation of great masses of the people—only the blind could ignore these ominous signs of a developing revolutionary situation. Complacent bourgeois Christians might persuade themselves that poverty was due to the thriftlessness of the poor or alternatively to the working of the inexorable laws of supply and demand. But men of truer insight and deeper feeling could not but be stirred to satisfy the needs, physical and spiritual, of the poor, and could not but sympathise with the political and social aspirations of the workers. Like Arnold Toynbee and Disraeli, Maurice could see the widening gulf between the classes and was resolved to do what in him lay to bridge it. His contributions were the Christian Socialist movement and the Working Men's College.

In this connection, we may find part, though only part, of the explanation of the action of Maurice which so puzzled Thomas Carlyle and J. S. Mill, namely his joining the Church of England and taking orders. To both Carlyle and Mill such a step seemed to involve intolerable intellectual compromise or a romantic idealising of a retrograde institution. In a letter in 1837, Carlyle wrote, 'I met Maurice in the Strand yesterday. He is growing broader, thicker and gets a clerical air. I know not why I should not wish him clerical or an English clergyman, yet I never do. His vehement earnestness in twisting such a rope of sand as I reckon that to be, occasions me at times a certain misgiving.' To John Stuart Mill it seemed clear that 'an established clergy must be the enemies to the progressiveness of the human mind'. So for Maurice to join their ranks was like deserting to the enemy. As he knew and respected Maurice the only way in which Mill could account for it was to assume in Maurice the same kind of distrust of private judgment as appears in Newman. 'I have never been able to find any other explanation of this than by attributing it to that timidity of conscience, combined with original sensitiveness of temperament which has so often driven highly gifted men into Romanism from the need of a firmer support than they can find in the independent conclusions of their own judgment.'[1] This explanation is kindly intentioned, but a close scrutiny of the reasons which led Maurice to join the Church of England does not bear it out. Beyond question, among those reasons was his awareness of a growing social cleavage in the nation, and his conviction that a national church might be indispensable to the maintenance or restoration of national unity. But this reason, important though it is, does not take us to the heart of Maurice's position.

In the next chapter I shall endeavour to indicate the deeper personal reasons which led him from Unitarianism to Anglicanism. I shall have something to say of the influences which guided him, and I shall outline his main principles as set forth in 'the Kingdom of Christ'. Continuing my reflections on Maurice's endeavours to find the secret of human life and the ends for which men should live, I shall illustrate the development and application of his principles from a selection of his writings mainly in chronological order.

I shall start with his criticism of Newman's theory of development, and show how he differed from Newman alike in their judgments as to the ultimate nature of Christianity and as to the course of development. Next in order I shall comment on one of the most popular of his writings, his lectures on the *Religions of the World*, in which he defines afresh the relation of Christianity to other

[1] *Autobiography* (World Classics edition), p. 130.

faiths. The *Theological Essays* will come next and will involve some discussion of his teaching on the Atonement and on Eternal Punishment. In the sixth chapter, I propose to examine his controversy with Mansel, on the fundamental question, What is Revelation? With the seventh chapter we shall turn to his contribution to education and social ethics. I shall deal first with *Learning and Working*, which may well rank with Newman's *Idea of a University*, as a classic on adult education. His critique of utilitarian ethics and his positive teaching on social morality in his *Cambridge Lectures* will next fall to be considered, and will lead on to a concluding assessment of the relevance of his teaching to the problems of to-day.

BIOGRAPHICAL APPENDIX TO CHAPTER I

I am not attempting to re-write the life of John Frederick Denison Maurice, but a brief chronological outline may be a convenience for reference. He was born at Normanstone in Suffolk on 29 August 1805, the only surviving son of Michael and Priscilla Maurice. He had three sisters older than himself —Elizabeth born in 1795, Mary in 1797, Anne in 1799; four younger—Emma (1807), Priscilla (1810) and twins, Esther and Lucilla. The date of their birth is not given in the authoritative biography of Maurice, but it was after the removal of the family to Frenchay, near Bristol, in 1813. Esther Maurice became the wife of Julius Hare in 1844. Owing to religious difficulties, Maurice decided to read for the Bar. He went up to Cambridge in 1823, and with Julius Hare as tutor read Classics at Trinity College. Along with John Sterling whom he came to know well, he migrated to Trinity Hall to read Law. He took a first-class in Civil Law in 1827, but left Cambridge without a degree as he was not at that time prepared to subscribe to the Articles. He went to London and engaged in journalism and literary work. During this period he wrote his one novel, *Eustace Conway*. The first draft was completed by 1830, but it was not published until 1834. He entered as a student at Exeter College, Oxford, at the beginning of 1830, and graduated with a second class in Classics in Michaelmas term, 1831. W. E. Gladstone was among his undergraduate friends in Oxford. His decision to go up to Oxford was determined by his desire to take orders. He was baptised on 29 March 1831, and he was ordained on 26 January 1834. For a short time, he held a curacy at Bubbenhall in Warwickshire. He was appointed chaplain at Guy's Hospital and came into residence there in 1836. This appointment enabled him to marry Anna Barton, sister-in-law of John Sterling, in 1837. There were two sons by this marriage, Edmund and Frederick. Unhappily, Maurice lost his wife in 1845. In 1840 he was appointed Professor of English Literature and History at King's College, London. In 1845 he delivered two series of lectures on 'The Religions of the World', when he held the position of Boyle and Warburton lecturer. In 1846 he was appointed to the chair of divinity at King's College. His initiative in 1847 led to the founding in the following year of Queen's College, the first of its kind for women. In 1848 he and Charles Kingsley, whom he had come to know in 1844, met the challenge of Chartism by issuing *Politics for the People* and by fostering Christian Socialism. A year or two earlier he resigned his position at Guy's Hospital to take up the chaplaincy of Lincoln's Inn, which he held from 1846 to 1860. In July 1849 he married Julius Hare's sister, Georgiana. The publication of his *Theological Essays* in 1853 led to his dismissal from his appointments at King's College. This was followed almost immediately by the invitation to Maurice to become Principal of the newly founded Working Men's College in 1854. He continued as Principal until his removal to Cambridge in 1866 on his election to the Knightbridge Professorship of Casuistry and Moral Philosophy. He held this professorial chair at the time of his death on 1 April 1872. He was incumbent of St Peter's, Vere Street, from 1860 to 1869. From 1870 to 1872 he was incumbent of St Edward's in Cambridge, in which church will be found an interesting memorial[1] to Maurice, though his connection with it was so brief. Augustine Birrell records that when he went up to Trinity Hall in 1869 'there being no room for me in college I was provided with rooms in St Edward's Passage, commanding a cheerful view of the small burial ground attached to St Edward's Church, a living in the gift of the Hall, and then occupied by that pious man, the Rev. F. D. Maurice, the author of countless books once widely read. . . . Sitting by my open window in St Edward's Passage, I could hear the beautiful and reverend voice of Maurice reading or rather reciting the Church services, which though verbally the same as those formerly conducted by Dr Farmer in his country church, were separated therefrom by a distance, "measureless to man".'[2]

---

[1] The text of the memorial is as follows:

FREDERICK DENISON MAURICE

1805–1872. Founder of the Working Men's College
and of the Queen's College for women in London.
Knightbridge Professor in Cambridge.

Chaplain of this Church where he spoke
his last words of love and sealed a life devoted
to the cause of truth and unity among Christians.
Faith was his in Christ, Eternal Hope
and Love.

[2] *Things past redress*, p. 63.

CHAPTER II

THE KINGDOM OF CHRIST

◆━━━◆

As we have seen, the Victorian era in religious thought is marked by a transference of interest and emphasis from the sovereignty to the fatherhood of God, from the doctrine of the Atonement to the doctrine of the Incarnation, from the concern for personal to the concern for social salvation. It was also the period of the movement back to Jesus, which in one aspect at least was a movement away from Paul. Then while many influences tended to raise men's conception of the Church and of the authority of the Church, there was also a definite trend away from religions of authority to the religion of experience. This last change of interest, one might say, begins in Great Britain with the emphasis of Coleridge and Thomas Erskine on the inward witness and enters on a new phase with William James's *Varieties of Religious Experience*.

To all these developments Maurice made a great contribution, though, as we shall see, neither singly nor taken together do these developments represent what was deepest and most characteristic in his thought and outlook. We have only to trace his influence on Baldwin Brown and John Hunter to see how much he meant to those who made the Fatherhood of God the centre of their faith and message. Martineau regarded Maurice as the chief cause of a radical and paramount change in the 'orthodox' theology, viz. the shifting of its centre of gravity from the Atonement to the Incarnation. Possibly Westcott in some ways best represents Maurice on this side. And it may fairly be said that Maurice stressed Johannine more than Pauline Christianity. Dr Mackennal thinks that Maurice's influence on Congregationalists was most effective in awakening the social consciousness and in delivering them from the narrow and excessive individualism of older Evangelicals and *laissez-faire* radicals. Gore and Scott Holland donned the mantle of Maurice, 'Christian Socialist', and perpetuated his tradition. Another sentence from Martineau, descriptive of the religious realism which he found in Coleridge and Maurice, discovers the strength of this school to lie 'in the faithful interpretation of what is at once deepest and highest in the religious consciousness, and its recognition, in this consciousness, of a living Divine person'. This indicates something of the significance of Maurice as one who enlarged men's understanding of the religion of experience. And Martineau comes very close to the deepest thing in Maurice when he refers to the recognition in men's religious consciousness of the presence or action of a living Divine person. But if, mistakenly, we treat as antithetical alternatives the Kingship and the Fatherhood of God, the Atonement and the Incarnation, individual salvation and social redemption, authority and experience, however much Maurice may have contributed to a change of emphasis or interest, in no case was he prepared to substitute the one for the other in these suggested alternatives. He did not so much direct men's thought from one doctrine to another as change their whole conception of doctrine. He did not pit one aspect of truth against another, but aimed at a genuine comprehension. He remoulded men's ideas of the kingdom of Christ and of their relation to it. The changes outlined were incidental to this more fundamental development.

To appreciate his position it is necessary to recall the experience and the influences which led to it. No one can write about Maurice without stressing his passionate desire for unity. He was born the son of a Unitarian minister, and as he wrote to J. M. Ludlow, 'in the fullest and best sense of the word I can be nothing else than a Unitarian—the pursuit of unity being the end which God has set before me from my cradle upwards'. Looking back on his life in 1871, he said, 'the desire for Unity and the search for Unity both in the nation and the Church has haunted me all my days'. The same passion for Unity drove him on from the Unitarianism in which he was cradled to the Anglicanism which he came to embrace.

Born in 1805, he was the only boy in a family of girls and he came midway in the family. Another boy died in infancy. During the later and longer part of his boyhood, the family lived in the neighbourhood of Bristol. No doubt his chivalry and his sensitiveness, perhaps his shyness also, were developed through the dominant influence of sisters. Intellectually, the independent minds of his older sisters and their freely expressed judgments affected him profoundly. His sisters and his mother gave up the Unitarianism of his father and felt unable to join in public worship with him. This break-up of the religious fellowship of his home circle engendered in Maurice his passion for unity. Presumably he would in any case have been led to criticise his father's religious position, because the saying attributed to Monsignor Ronald Knox, 'I must have a religion but it must be different from father's', has in some degree at least, a universal application. But the boy owed much to his father, and he himself realised the extent of his debt. The Rev. Michael Maurice had been trained at Hoxton when that academy was under the powerful influence of Dr Priestley. Indeed he knew and admired Priestley. But while he became a Unitarian, more or less of Priestley's school, he was not a hard dogmatic Unitarian, nor did he accept the necessarian outlook of Priestley and Hartley from which Martineau had no small exercise of mind to free himself. Michael Maurice shared something of the older non-subscribing tradition, which the Rev. J. M. Lloyd Thomas revived during his ministry at the Old Meeting House in Birmingham. Michael Maurice used the Trinitarian formula in baptism, on which practice Robert Hall, who knew him well, observed, 'Why, sir, as I understand you, you must consider that you baptise in the name of an abstraction, a man and a metaphor.' Maurice's father was satisfied with the scriptural authority for the formula, and was not concerned to harmonise his practice with the divinity he had learnt at Hoxton. Maurice says of his father that he believed in the Bible more strongly and passionately than most of his sect and was an enthusiastic champion of the Bible Society. Michael Maurice was tolerant of honest differences of opinion, willing to co-operate with more orthodox Christians, indignant when co-operation was declined, and apt to be impatient with those who could not see what seemed reasonable and obvious to him. With considerable modifications, all these characteristics reappear in his son.[1] The father also initiated the son in the Whig-Liberal tradition in politics.

[1] Mrs Brookfield confirms the judgment of Dean Church at this point. In writing to Thackeray, she compared Maurice with Pusey, and said, 'Mr Maurice has the same sweeping mode of setting before you what he means, as if there were no question that you must agree if only you have sense to understand!' See *Mrs Brookfield and her circle*, p. 312.

Both his mother and father were active in good causes and in all that concerned the social welfare of the people. The germs of Christian Socialism were planted in the mind and heart of the growing boy. His dissatisfaction with his father's creed was due first to the fact that it ceased to satisfy his mother and his sisters, and second that it was not confirmed by his own reading and study of the Scriptures. The Calvinism which his mother and sisters embraced did not satisfy him either, though he could see that they had found in Calvinism truths to which Unitarianism had not done justice. He did not feel disposed simply to follow his sisters. He was seeking some way of combining what was true in either Unitarianism or Calvinism, though he did not at once discover the principle which was to determine his approach to all problems of philosophical and religious thought. The development of his sisters' church attachments also affected him. For while Elizabeth, the eldest, joined the Church of England, Anne and Mary followed the ministry of John Foster, the essayist, at the Baptist Chapel in Vernon Street, Bristol. John Foster, who is credited with possessing an equal facility in emptying pews and filling heads, retained the interest of these young women and made them staunch dissenters. The problem of Church versus Dissent was thus presented to the boy in his immediate family circle. He himself heard and admired both John Foster and Robert Hall, and it would be interesting to enquire whether they did not exert a stronger formative influence on his growing mind than has as yet been recognised.

While the divisions in the family compelled him to think critically about the religion of his father, his own study of the Bible led him to the conviction that there was much more in the religion of the Bible than had found expression in the Unitarian tradition. To his boyish logic, he tells us, Unitarianism seemed incoherent and feeble. He was brought up to believe in the Fatherhood of God, and he found the doctrine, as presented to him, too shallow. He did not correct or repudiate the sternness of Calvinism, by affirming the Fatherhood of God. It would be truer to say that he deepened an inadequate conception of the benevolence of God by reinterpreting Fatherhood in the light which Calvinism threw on the nature of sin and the need of Atonement. He was brought up to believe in forgiveness without atonement and he could not rest satisfied with any such position. It seemed to him that Unitarianism offered us a God above the battle, and this meant an emasculated gospel. 'It was reserved for this religion', he says in the *Kingdom of Christ* (1, p. 146) 'to make it the greatest evidence and proof of love in a Divine Being that He merely pardons those who have filled the world with misery: that He has never shared in it: never wrestled with it: never devised any means, save that of sending a wise teacher, for delivering mankind out of it.' If he felt that the substitutionary view of the Atonement was also wrong, it was not because he made light of the Atonement, but because the traditional doctrine seemed to him a travesty of the truth. Similarly, he was brought up to believe in universalism and to deny eternal torment, and he came to realise that the hope and the denial were both too lightly asserted.

I was brought up in the belief of universal restitution; I was taught that the idea of eternal punishment could not consist with the goodness and mercy of God. When I came to think and feel for myself, I began to suspect these determinations.

It did not seem to me that the views I had learnt respecting sin accorded with my experience of it, or with the facts which I saw in the world. I had a certain revolting, partly of intellect and partly of conscience, against what struck me as a feeble notion of the Divine perfections, one which represented *good nature* as the highest of them. Nor could I acquiesce in the unfair distortions of the text of Scripture by which, as I thought, they justified their conclusions; for I had always learnt to reverence the Scriptures, not to set them aside. I did not see how αἰώνιος could mean one thing when it was joined with κόλασις, and another when it was joined with ζωή.

I do not mean that these were very deep, vital *convictions*; they were honest *opinions* as far as they went, though mixed with much intellectual pride. I despised the Universalist and Unitarian as weak; I do not know that I found anything at all better.[1]

His eventual challenge to the orthodox doctrine of Eternal Punishment was the fruit of the moral and intellectual travail of one who was resolved not to make light of sin or its punishment.

The movement of Maurice's mind was constantly misunderstood in his own day and has frequently been misrepresented since. A single example may serve as illustration. In 1864, Dr Liddon refused Dean Stanley's invitation to preach at the Abbey, because Maurice among others had been invited also. Dr Liddon wrote, 'It is only by his books and by his letters in the newspapers that I know anything of Mr F. D. Maurice. That he is so good a man I rejoice to believe with all my heart. It is an earnest of his return to the faith of the Church. That so good a man should be mistaken is a very perplexing mystery in the moral world. But he is not its

---

[1] *Life of F. D. Maurice*, II, 15. A passage from a letter to F. J. A. Hort.

only illustration. No one doubts Channing's goodness, yet Channing taught Socinianism in terms.' Such a letter seems to suggets that to Liddon Maurice appeared as one drifting from orthodoxy to Socinianism instead of one moving in the reverse direction, as if Maurice were seeking to bring the Church into line with Channing, instead of seeking to win Channing over to the Church.[1] Maurice in theology was essentially conservative and constructive. That is why his criticism of traditional orthodoxy was so effective and so resented. But I must hasten on to speak of some of the major formative influences which helped to determine his outlook in early manhood.

Clearly, the tuition and friendship of Julius Hare at Cambridge meant much to him. In particular Hare introduced him to Plato. I suspect that from this tuition he arrived at the principle of the polarity of truth—the principle that truth is often manifested in apparently opposing forms. He might indeed have learned it from Charles Simeon, for, as Dr C. H. Smyth points out, 'To Simeon belongs the grand discovery, so naturally disconcerting to the English mind, that "the truth is not in the middle and not in one extreme: but in both extremes".' But probably Maurice was, in this matter, a disciple of Plato, and learned his lesson from the Sophist, where we read, 'The philosopher who has the truest reverence for these qualities (knowledge, reason, mind)

[1] Dr F. J. Powicke records that Edward White took Liddon's view of the trend of Maurice's influence. 'He, Edward White, was very emphatic, not to say, truculent in the assertion of his belief that its chief effect was to produce Unitarians.' Dr Powicke wrote to Edward White privately to assure him that, on the contrary, Maurice had saved him from Unitarianism. Edward White then characterised Maurice-ianism as a half-way house on the road to and from orthodoxy, from and to Unitarianism! (*Congregational Quarterly*, April 1930, pp. 175 f.)

cannot possibly accept the notion of those who say the whole is at rest, either as unity or in many forms: he will be utterly deaf to those who assert universal motion. As children say entreatingly, "Give us both", so he will include both the moveable and immoveable in his definition of being and all.' But Maurice certainly agreed with Simeon in rejecting the Englishman's tendency to compromise—the tendency, described by Newman, as seeking a way between right and wrong down the channel of no-meaning. J. S. Mill wrote more restrainedly of the Englishman's highly salutary shrinking from all extremes. 'But,' he says, 'as this shrinking is rather an instinct of caution than a result of insight, it is too ready to satisfy itself with any medium, merely because it is a medium and to acquiesce in a union of the disadvantages of both extremes instead of their advantages.' Maurice was anxious to do justice to both extremes, to combine the advantages of both, as the result of insight. He abhors eclecticism, though he may not always succeed in avoiding it. But armed with this discovery of the polarity of truth, he examined the divisions of the Christian Church, expecting to find that men are normally right in what they affirm and wrong in what they deny. Obviously things will not work out quite as simply as that, but Maurice was most concerned to expose the errors of those who find truth in only one extreme and who proceed to erect systems and organise churches on their limited discovery. It may be noted that in applying this principle of the polarity of truth, Maurice did not follow the Hegelian dialectic, though he would not have found it altogether uncongenial. But perhaps he would have regarded synthesis not as a recurrent stage in a dialectical movement but as an endeavour of perpetual obligation. In any case, a true Catholicity was only to be achieved by finding the truth in extremes. The œcumenical movement can proceed only on this assumption and by this method.

Another reflection of the influence of Plato may be found in the distinction which Maurice drew between principles on the one hand and notions or opinions on the other. This distinction puzzled his admirers. Miss Williams Wynn, a clever member of Mrs Brookfield's circle, writes on one occasion, 'We heard an uncommonly good sermon from Maurice, the best I ever listened to of his, and he only got once into an unintelligible difficulty about notional truth as opposed to truth untainted by our notions. How we are to get at it at present without such taint, I did not make out.'[1] Leslie Stephen is equally at sea. Ordinary common sense, he tells us, was perplexed by Maurice's statements as to the worthlessness of mere dogmas or opinions as such, and their infinite value when considered as divine revelations of truth. Plato's belief in Ideas, coupled with his reluctance to define them might have given the lady and Leslie Stephen the clue to this unintelligible difficulty. Maurice was always urging folk to stick to their principles, for to him principles had the independent reality of Platonic ideas. But just as Socrates is convinced of the reality of justice, though he cannot define it, so we should distinguish between the principles, of the truth of which we are convinced, and the particular notions or opinions in which we formulate our conceptions of those principles. Assuming the validity of this distinction, Maurice could say, 'cling to principles', 'sit loose to notions or opinions'. He believed men constantly entered into controversy, not so much for principles

[1] *Mrs Brookfield and her circle*, p. 278.

as for opinions, and he believed there was less real opposition between principles than there was between opinions.

Maurice's debt to Coleridge was even greater than his debt to Plato, and he has estimated it generously in dedicating his first work, *The Kingdom of Christ*, to Derwent Coleridge. The sub-title, *Hints on the Nature of the Catholic Church*, may have been suggested by Coleridge's *Aids to Reflection*. From Coleridge he learned some of his fundamental ideas on the nature of society, which we will take up in the concluding chapter. Coleridge confirmed his insistence on principles and taught him that principles or ultimate truths are presupposed in experience rather than derived from it and also are such that they appeal to the peasant as well as to the scholar. This conviction as to the appeal of ultimate truths inspired his work in adult education, and determined the lines of his preaching. But in some ways more important than these convictions was his attitude to history. He says that Coleridge taught him to revere the facts of history. The facts of history for Maurice were not the clear-cut data which the American student is apt to seek and absorb endlessly. Canon Farrar who as a youth attended Maurice's lectures on history at King's College shows how the lecturer's reverence for facts appeared to irreverent students. Farrar wrote to Maurice's son and biographer, 'I remember a clever student writing a parody of one of your father's lectures which made us all laugh. It began, "The fourteenth century was preceded by the thirteenth and followed by the fifteenth. This is *a deep fact*. It is not indeed one of those facts which find their way into popular compendiums, but etc." But while we laughed good-humouredly, some of us felt that our debt to our teacher was far too deep to be shaken by such a caricature of his style and method.' For the facts which students love, dates and names and what not, the King's College men had to go to Maurice's assistant. But events and the sequence of events seemed to Maurice to be full of meaning. Leslie Stephen observed rightly that 'the peculiarity which divided Maurice from the mystics was his strong conviction of the necessity of an historical element in theology'. Maurice saw clearly that the appeal of the Bible to ordinary folk is due to the fact that here we have religion in history. He also saw, what has since become a commonplace, though unintelligible to Leslie Stephen and common sense in the 1870's, that divine revelations of truth will be given to us in events and not in dogmatic propositions.[1] But this brings us to his most profound conviction, this, namely, that the revelation of God must come through a personal mediator, that the Church can find unity only in a personal centre, and that the world

[1] The following sentences from *The Kingdom of Christ*, I, 196, state the essential point clearly: '... the revelation which the reason demands, cannot be one of merely moral principles or axioms—it must be the revelation of a living Being. It cannot therefore be one in which events are merely accidents that can be separated from some idea which has tried to embody itself in them. Facts may be only the drapery of *doctrines*: but they would seem to be the only possible method of manifestation of the Being, the essential Reason.'

How much in advance of his own time Maurice was, and how closely he anticipated present-day appreciation of Christianity as asserting the revelation of the Eternal God in history and in a specific history—the life, death and resurrection of Jesus Christ—the reader can gauge by consulting the opening chapters of Professor L. Hodgson's book *The Doctrine of the Trinity* and of Professor C. H. Dodd's *History and the Gospel*. Compare also this passage from C. R. North, *The Old Testament Interpretation of History*, p. 153: 'We grant that the ideas have been mediated through history and we are scrupulously careful, when we expound them, to place them in their historical setting. We fail to see that the historical circumstances are an integral part of the revelation.... In point of fact, the historical occasion is an essential element in the revelation.'

34

can find unity and salvation only in realising that the kingdom of Christ is already established in the earth. He never used the terms, but Maurice was the convinced exponent of both Biblical realism and realised eschatology.[1]

The remarkable letter which he wrote to his father after he had joined the Church of England is too long to quote, but it is the finest and clearest expression of the faith by which he lived. He finds in the records of the saints and heroes of the Old Testament a recognition of God as incomprehensible and infinite coupled with a longing to understand and comprehend that same God. He is sure that human nature cries out for a reconciliation of these two amazing contrarieties.

If this be the one great cry of human nature in all ages, just in proportion as it was enlightened, then cannot any explanation be found for it except only that which will satisfy it. If the Infinite Incomprehensible Jehovah is manifested in the person of a Man, a Man conversing with us, living among us, entering into all our infirmities and temptations, and passing into all our conditions, it is satisfied; if not, it remains unsatisfied. Man is still dealing with an incomprehensible Being, without any mode of comprehending Him. He may be revealed to him as his lawgiver, his sovereign, but he has no means of knowing Him as a friend.

The promised revelation has been given to us in Jesus Christ. This is the Gospel.

In arriving at his conception of the Kingdom of Christ, Maurice was much helped by the writings of Thomas

[1] For the nature and meaning of Biblical Realism, the reader should consult Dr Kraemer's impressive book *The Christian Message in a non-Christian World*.

'Realised eschatology' is expounded in more than one of Professor C. H. Dodd's works.

Erskine, particularly it would seem by *The Brazen Serpent*.
He was introduced to the writings of Thomas Erskine, by
Bruce, eighth Earl of Elgin, when they were undergraduates together at Oxford. But this was not the
beginning of Erskine's influence upon him. When his
mother embraced Calvinism, she could not convince
herself that she was among the elect. This caused a deep
depression in the mind of her son, who was then in his
teens. He took a similar gloomy view of his own prospects,
and in writing to a lady whom he knew described himself
as 'a being destined to a few short years of misery here,
as an earnest of and preparation for that more enduring
state of wretchedness and woe', etc. Fortunately the lady
was a disciple of Thomas Erskine. She wrote back,
'Where is your authority for regarding any individual of
the human race as *destined* to misery either here or hereafter? Such a view is not supported by the letter or the
spirit of that revelation which alone can be admitted as
evidence in the case.'[1]

Mr Sanders seems to think that Maurice learnt from
Erskine the doctrine of the absolute sovereignty of God.
He says, 'To Thomas Erskine Maurice expressed his
gratitude for teaching him not to forget the Calvinistic
doctrine that the God of both individuals and nations has
infinite power.'[2] But Maurice had accepted this doctrine
before he heard of Erskine. It was the teaching of Erskine
which helped him to retain a belief in the sovereignty of
God while rejecting the doctrine of reprobation. But as
he makes clear in the dedication of *Prophets and Kings*,
his debt to Erskine was something much more than this.
He owed to Erskine his conviction of the universality of
the Gospel and his mystical theory of Christ's Divine

[1] *Life*, I, 43.   [2] *Coleridge and the Broad Church Movement*, p. 185.

Headship of humanity. He writes in the dedication, 'Have we a Gospel for men, for all men? Is it a Gospel that God's will is a will to all Good, a will to deliver them from all Evil? Is it a Gospel that He has reconciled the world to Himself? Is it this absolutely, or this with a multitude of reservations, explanations, contradictions?' Then he adds, addressing Erskine, 'It is more than twenty years (written in 1853) since a book of yours brought home to my mind the conviction that no Gospel but this can be of any use to the world, and that the Gospel of Jesus Christ is such a one.' The book in question was *The Brazen Serpent*. In it Erskine affirmed a necessary and eternal connection between Christ and humanity. H. F. Henderson summarises the main thought in these words.

Human nature, though composed of many members, is viewed in its totality as one organic body, of which Christ is the Head and Representative. To quote from *The Brazen Serpent*: 'The whole nature is as one colossal man, of which Christ continues the Head during the whole accepted time and day of salvation.' If we ask what were the benefits secured to our race absolutely and unconditionally through this eternal connection of Christ with it, his reply is, that the absolute and unconditional benefits are two in number, namely, forgiveness and immortality. Again, to those who fulfil the condition of faith, 'this is the great thing which Christ has accomplished by suffering for us—He has become a Head of new and un-condemned life to every man in the light of which we may see God's love in the law and the punishment, and may thus suffer to the glory of God and draw out from the suffering that blessing which is contained in it.'[1]

Here is the germ of Maurice's conception of the King-dom of Christ as actual and all-embracing. It will be

---

[1] H. F. Henderson, *Erskine of Linlathen*, p. 60.

remembered that Dr Dale arrived independently at a somewhat similar conception of Christ as the Head and Representative of mankind.[1] The conception reflects the teaching of St Paul in Romans v. Christ, the Second Adam, by his obedience unto death, has brought mercy to mankind as surely as the first Adam by disobedience brought death into the world. So Christ is not only the head of a new humanity: he has changed the moral situation for all men. This conviction inspires Maurice's book on the Kingdom of Christ. Christ is the head of every man, though they neither know nor acknowledge Him. The task of the Church is to bring this truth home to men.

The Kingdom of Christ was published in its present form in 1842. It was a refashioning of a series of twelve letters to a Quaker, which had been published in 1838 and are now hard to come by. It is quite impossible to convey an adequate impression in a single chapter either of the original letters or of the later treatise. It will serve, however, to illustrate his principles and his method if I say something first of Maurice's discussion of Quakerism and second of his position as a member of the Church of England.

As may be expected, Maurice's interpretations of other folks' convictions seldom satisfy other folks. Dr Mackennal found the account of the early Independents in *The Kingdom of Christ* painful reading, and undoubtedly it is inadequate. Somewhat similarly, I think Maurice failed to appreciate something very vital in primitive Quakerism. He has no adequate understanding of worship after the manner of Friends, the discovery of silence as the way of wonder, and the recovery of the spontaneous prophetic

[1] See the discussion and comparison of the teaching of Maurice and Dale on Christ the Head of a new Humanity, in Mackennal, *Evolution of Congregationalism*, pp. 195–206.

ministry. But Maurice saw very clearly many elements of strength and weakness in Quakerism and in some respects he understood Friends better than they understood or understand themselves. He was writing to a Friend, who subsequently took orders, but who at the time was troubled by the Beacon controversy which occupied Friends very considerably about 1835. The Beacon controversy in this country was the counterpart and echo of the much more disastrous Hicksite controversy which split the Society in America in 1827. In brief, the controversy was a clash between fundamentalist Evangelicals who in effect repudiated the primitive Quaker belief in the inward light, and more conservative Quakers who distrusted Evangelical theology as inconsistent with the original Quaker faith. In the upshot a small minority of ultra-evangelical Friends left the Society and joined the Plymouth Brethren and other bodies. Maurice was fully aware of the significance of the controversy. In it, as he saw, the primitive Quaker and the Evangelical were parting company. It was a mistake, for each needs the other. He urges his correspondent not to abandon Friends' principles, but to consider whether Quakerism, as a system based on those principles, can possibly be an adequate witness to the Gospel.

He characterises the founder of the Society of Friends in the following terms. 'I consider George Fox a great man and an eminent teacher. Do not mistake me. I do not think George Fox had a commission to preach the gospel. I do not think that in the strict sense of the word, he did preach the gospel: but I think that he was raised up to declare a truth without which the gospel has no real meaning, no permanent existence.' In the original letter Maurice gave his interpretation of the inner light. 'Fox perceives that man is a twofold creature: that there is a power always drawing him down to which he is naturally subject and to be subject to which is death: but that there is also a power drawing him up, a light shining in darkness and that to yield to that power, to dwell in that light, is life and peace.' This is no fanatical or mystical belief. 'Mysticism glorifies its own feelings and ambitions: but Fox considered that the revelation to himself was only the discovery of a truth which belonged to all his brethren.' He was witnessing to the presence of a Divine Word in the conscience.

I do not think this interpretation of Fox's main principle would be disputed, though it has more facets, more sides to it than appear in such a summary. But the doctrine, so interpreted, Maurice sees clearly is not Christianity. Fox's doctrine does not do justice to three great ideas of Christianity—the justification of the conscience, the atonement for mankind, and the Trinity. By justification of the conscience Maurice seems to have meant the condemnation of sin and the assurance of forgiveness which the awakened conscience requires. But the essential point is that there is no inward Christ apart from an outward Christ. Christ *for* us and Christ *in* us are inseparable. Without the inward light, the gospel remains a dead letter, an idle notion, but without the gospel, the inward light has no proper sustaining power, no full glory. Compare the sentence 'The religious experience without the vision of History would be empty, the historical event without the religious experience blind.' The inward light varies in character and intensity according as it is understood to be the presupposition of the gospel, the inward witness without which the gospel can never be understood or welcomed, or to be the outcome of the gospel, the contemporary inspiration of the Holy Spirit, the divine guidance of believers. It is the weakness of Friends that they often fail to distinguish these varying intensities of inward illumination, and claim for the first the glory of the second, and even on occasion treat the presupposition as if it were the gospel or a substitute for the gospel. Maurice, on the other hand, did not realise how far Fox's teaching on the inward light took the gospel for granted. But his critique of Quakerism is an excellent example of his method of bringing together complementary truths, which should never be opposed to one another or separated from one another.

His detailed observations show a real acquaintance with the state of the Society in his day, and they are not irrelevant to the Society of to-day. Thus he questioned, as others within and without the Society are questioning now, whether the range of Friends' testimony was not too narrow, whether they were bearing an adequate testimony against profit-seeking and mammon-worship—the real moral perils of the age—and whether their testimony against all war could be valid or effective without a further testimony against the worldliness of economic man. Maurice also detected or thought he detected an inconsistency in Friends rejecting a recognised paid ministry while employing a large number of teachers. He asks very pertinently, why should paid teachers be spiritual, if paid ministers are not? Early Friends, in denouncing a hireling ministry—a ministry maintained by the compulsory payment of tithe—did not sufficiently envisage the fact that a man might be called to give himself to the full-time work of the ministry and depend legitimately on the provision the Church makes for his maintenance. To denounce all paid ministry as hireling and unspiritual is a quite untenable position for a Christian.

From time to time one detects among Friends an anti-clerical prejudice which hinders fellowship and co-operation with our fellow Christians. Maurice laid his finger on a real weakness. Yet it is to be hoped that as long as the distinct existence of the Society of Friends is of service to Christ and His Church, it will continue as essentially an embodiment of lay Christianity. It is to be hoped that London Yearly Meeting will not succumb to the temptation to adopt the pastoral system which prevails in some Yearly Meetings in America. Friends have to witness to the priesthood of all believers, to the responsibility of all members of the Church for the right holding of meetings for worship and for the publication of truth. And in any case the presence of a robust lay Christianity may help to correct excesses of professionalism and sacerdotalism in the Christian ministry.

The consideration of the ministry makes a natural transition to Maurice's position as a member of the Church of England, for one point in which he held the Church to be right and the Quakers mistaken was in recognising that if an inward call is essential to the ministry, proper recognition or ordination is also necessary.

The orders and sacraments of the Church of England appealed to him. Indeed, in his views on apostolic succession and ministerial authority, he was not far removed from the standpoint of the Oxford Movement. It is not too much to say that the liturgy and the standards of the Anglican church captured his mind and heart. Even wholehearted admirers failed to appreciate his attitude. The reactions of J. S. Mill and Thomas Carlyle are readily understood, but even John Hunter, who owed so much to Maurice, was at one time puzzled by his Anglicanism.

Dean Stanley, Kingsley and Maurice I held and hold in high esteem and I am in full sympathy with their general theological position, but it is precisely their attitude in regard to the doctrinal beliefs and liturgical forms by which they were bound as servants of the State which makes me wholly sceptical as to the healthy liberalising influence in the long run of their Church. Their efforts to reconcile modern thought with formularies of belief and worship belonging to a condition of mind and feeling which were quite alien to these times were a melancholy waste of power.[1]

John Hunter wrote this in 1885, and later in his life he felt somewhat differently. Perhaps he should not have bracketed Stanley and Maurice. Carlyle sensed a difference when he described Maurice as weaving ropes of sand and denounced Stanley for knocking holes in the bottom of the Church of England. This suggests that Maurice was conservative and constructive, while Stanley was liberalising and loosening, if not destructive. But explain it how we will, Maurice sincerely accepted the creeds. He regarded the Articles, not as containing the answers to all questions but as a sound definition of the attitude of the Church to the live issues of the sixteenth century and so as a guide in spirit rather than in detail to the attitude she should assume in the controversies of to-day. He valued the liturgical forms precisely because they were not modern, because the Book of Common Prayer is a book in which we join in prayers that unite us with praying souls of every Christian generation.[2] Maurice was not forcing his thought into alien forms. He loved the liturgy. His volume of sermons on the Prayer Book and the Lord's Prayer and the little book, *The Church a Family*, should

---

[1] *John Hunter*, by L. S. Hunter, p. 71.
[2] Compare R. D. Richardson, *Conflict of Ideals*, pp. 34, 35.

stand beside Hooker, Book v. Martineau reports one of
the best of the London clergy as saying 'The only man I
have ever known who really prayed the prayers was F. D.
Maurice.' His reading of the service attracted worshippers
to Lincoln's Inn Chapel at least as much as his preaching
and perhaps more than his preaching. There is a tribute
to Maurice at Lincoln's Inn from the pen of R. H. Hutton
which is worthy to stand beside J. A. Froude's tribute to
Newman in St Mary's.

It is about forty years since my most intimate friend, the
late Walter Bagehot, who was then a student at Lincoln's
Inn where he was afterwards called to the bar, took me to
hear one of the afternoon sermons of the chaplain of the Inn.
I remember Bagehot telling me, with his usual caution, that he
would not exactly answer for my being impressed by the
sermon, but that at all events he thought I should feel that
something different went on there from that which goes on in
an ordinary church or chapel service; that there was a sense
of 'something religious'—a phrase Maurice himself would
hardly have appreciated—in the air which was not to be
found elsewhere. I went, and it is hardly too much to say
that the voice and manner of the preacher—his voice and
manner in the reading-desk at least as much as in the pulpit—
have lived in my memory ever since, as no other voice and
manner have ever lived in it. The half-stern, half-pathetic
emphasis with which he gave the words of the Confession
'And there is *no* health in *us*,' throwing the weight of the
meaning on to the last word, and the rising of his voice into a
higher plane of hope as he passed away from the confession of
weakness to the invocation of God's help, struck the one note
of his life—the passionate trust in eternal help—as it had never
been struck in my hearing before. There was intensity—
almost too thrilling—and something, too, of sad exultation in
every tone, as if the reader were rehearsing a story in which
he had no part except his personal certainty of its truth, his

gratitude that it should be true, and his humiliation that it had fallen to such lips as his to declare it. This was what made his character present itself so strongly to the mind as almost embodied in *a voice*. He seemed to be the channel for a communication, not the source of it. There was a gentle hurry, and yet a peremptoriness, in those at once sad and sonorous tones, which spoke of haste to tell their tale, and of actual fear of not telling it with sufficient emphasis and force. 'They hurried on as if impatient to fulfil their mission.' They seemed put into his mouth, while he, with his whole soul bent on their wonderful drift, uttered them as an awestruck but thankful envoy tells the tale of danger and deliverance. Yet though Mr Maurice's voice seemed to be the essential part of him as a religious teacher, his face, if you ever looked at it, was quite in keeping with his voice. His eye was full of sweetness, but fixed, and, as it were, fascinated on some ideal point. His countenance expressed nervous, high-strung tension, as though all the various play of feelings in ordinary human nature converged, in him, towards a single focus—the declaration of the divine purpose.'[1]

Membership in any church with clearly defined standards is bound to involve individuals in some difficulties. But the sincerity and intellectual honesty of Maurice in his adhesion to the Church of England are beyond question. He perhaps more than any other of his contemporaries might legitimately be described as Anglo-Catholic, and the paradox of such a description would to his mind have been but one more example of the polarity of truth. He believed in the Church of England because it was national and comprehensive as no sect could be. He believed in the Church of England, because it seemed to him to present the claims of the church universal

[1] R. H. Hutton, *Modern Guides of English Thought in Matters of Faith*, pp. 316, 317.

effectively to the English people, and to enable the English people to take their rightful place in the church universal. The Church of Rome seemed to him to have erred fatally in claiming that the Pope was the vicar of Christ. Christ as Head of the Church does not delegate His authority to any visible representative. The true nature of the Catholic Church and of Christ's authority in His Church was, he held, better understood in the Church of England than in the Church of Rome.

He believed that the time was at hand when 'we may again have one Church throughout Christendom—a Church the parts of which will be nationally and universally united under their true Head, instead of being confounded under a pope or separated into sects'. He believed the Church of England had a unique contribution to make to this end. I do not think he was mistaken.

CHAPTER III

NEWMAN'S ESSAY ON DEVELOPMENT AND MAURICE'S CRITIQUE THEREOF

ON 9 October 1845 John Henry Newman was received into the Roman Catholic Church. A day later he added a memorable postscript to the manuscript of his *Essay on the Development of Christian Doctrine*. It ran thus:

Such were the thoughts concerning the 'Blessed Vision of Peace' of one whose long-continued petition had been that the Most High would not despise the work of His own hands, nor leave him to himself: while yet his eyes were dim, and his breast laden, and he could but employ Reason in the things of Faith. And now, dear reader, time is short, eternity is long. Put not from you what you have found here: regard it not as mere matter of controversy: set not out resolved to refute it and looking about for the best way of doing so: seduce not yourself with the imagination that it comes of disappointment, or disgust, or restlessness, or wounded feeling, or undue sensibility, or other weakness. Wrap not yourself round in the associations of years past, nor determine that to be truth which you wish to be so, nor make an idol of cherished anticipations. Time is short, eternity is long. Nunc dimittis servum tuum, Domine, secundum verbum tuum in pace quia viderunt oculi mei salutare tuum.

The primary interest of the essay may always turn on its place in Newman's religious history. As Dr Fairbairn said, 'The book was in the strictest possible sense an

47

earlier "Apologia pro vita sua"'. It was not, however, like the *Apologia*, a reply to critics. It was an explanation addressed to friends and enquirers. The essay set forth the considerations which convinced Newman that the Anglican Via Media was untenable and that he could only retain the full truth of the Christian faith by submitting to the authority of the Church of Rome. The memorable paragraph with which he closed his book is an appeal to his friends to follow his example.

Important as marking the great turning-point in Newman's spiritual pilgrimage, the *Essay* is hardly less important as stimulating thought on fundamental issues in the history of Christian faith. Since religion is concerned with that which is eternal and unchanging, it is natural that creeds, rites, and institutions should be maintained with an almost rigid conservatism. Rome boasts herself to be *semper eadem*, while successive Protestant denominations claim to reproduce primitive Christianity. But growth, or development, or evolution is inevitable. Rome has changed, and the Protestant claim to reproduce primitive Christianity intact is an illusion. 'Here below to live is to change, and to be perfect is to have changed often.' Two problems emerge, one for the historian, the other for the believer. The historian has to account for all existing forms of Christianity. He has to study Christianity in the light of its evolution, to distinguish and measure the factors which have promoted variety in interpretation and organisation. The believer is confronted with a further question. For him the original gospel is the vital thing. If the doctrines in which it is set forth must be subject to a process of development, how is he to distinguish legitimate necessary developments from corruptions or perversions? Or it may be, he should envisage the problem somewhat differently. All existing developments may be more or less legitimate, more or less corrupt. Which then is the richer and truer, and is it possible to combine elements of different Church-traditions in a larger whole?

The historian's problem and the believer's problem or problems are distinct, yet closely connected. Newman posed the historical question, but he was more concerned to answer the question of the believer. He did indeed give a great stimulus to historical study. Dr Fairbairn's brilliant survey of the law of development in Theology and the Church, in the first division of his *Christ in Modern Theology*, starts from a critique of Newman's *Essay*. While Newman cannot be held responsible for his conclusions, the seed of Loisy's daring modernist apologetic for Catholicism was sown when von Hügel introduced him to Newman's writings. Some features of the *Essay on Development* are of permanent value for historians, but in the main it is an essay in aid of faith and in commendation of a particular form of Christian faith.

To appreciate Newman's position and Maurice's critique of it, it will be necessary to outline the argument of the book. After defining ideas as habitual judgments—real if they represent existing facts, and imaginary if they stand for nothing external to themselves—Newman deprecates any attempt to reduce Christianity to a single idea.

Sometimes an attempt is made to ascertain the 'leading idea' as it has been called, of Christianity; a remarkable essay as directed towards a divine religion, when, even in the instance of the works of man, the task is beyond us. Thus, the one idea of the Gospel has been decided by some to be the restoration of our fallen race, by others philanthropy, by others spirituality of true religious service, by others the salvation of the elect, by others the union of the soul with God. All these representations are truths, as being aspects of Christianity but none of them is the whole truth. For Christianity has many aspects: it has its imaginative side, its philosophical, its ethical, its political: it is solemn and it is cheerful: it is indulgent and it is strict: it is light and it is dark: it is love and it is fear.[1]

This passage may well have suggested Loisy's criticism of Harnack's identification of the essence of Christianity with one leading idea or even with three leading ideas.

After distinguishing various kinds of development—physical, logical, historical and metaphysical among others—Newman enunciates his famous tests to distinguish legitimate developments from corruptions. They are, Preservation of Type or Idea, Continuity of Principles, Power of Assimilation, Early Anticipation, Logical Sequence, Preservative Addition, Chronic Continuance. Of these tests, perhaps the second and third have special interest. By continuity of principles Newman seems to have understood general character as contrasted with particular doctrines. The same doctrines may be held on different principles and the resultant doctrines will have a different ethos. One suspects that this is the reason why Tract XC failed to satisfy its author. To show that Tridentine definitions might be harmonised with the Thirty-nine Articles of the Church of England was not a sedative for Roman fever. The High Churchman might hold and teach the same doctrines as the Roman Catholic, but in the Church of England, he would hold and teach them on the principle of private judgment and it is only in the Roman Church that they would be held and taught on the basis of submission to an adequate authority. The

[1] *Essay*, p. 35.

case is similar with liturgical offices, as Tyrrell found when he attended the blessing of palms on Palm Sunday, first in an Anglican Church and then in a Roman Catholic chapel. In the first it felt like a daring innovation, an act of defiance of the tradition of the Church of England. In the second it was pervaded by the sense of continuity reaching back to the catacombs. The same service, but inspired by different principles! If the same doctrines may be held on different principles, different and even opposite doctrines may be arrived at on the basis of the same principle. Newman chooses as his example, the possibility that scepticism and Romanism may be held on the common conviction that there is no tenable intellectual position between the two. Thus it will be seen that the second test adds something essential to the first.

The third test, the power of assimilation, most nearly anticipates theories of development through adaptation to environment. Clearly the Christian faith must come to terms with culture and will be affected profoundly by the social and economic environment and by changes in that environment. Can Christianity absorb important elements of the cultural traditions with which it comes into contact without losing its own specific genius? Can it adapt itself to its social and economic environment without losing its character as the salt of the world? The power of assimilation must be the power to transmute as well as to absorb, the power to refashion the environment as well as to respond to it. The risk involved in the attempt to assimilate is as manifest as the futility of trying to keep Christianity pure by despising culture and holding aloof from the world.

This particular test is closely associated with the section on the probability of the developments in Christianity.

Newman might with propriety have asserted the necessity or inevitability of development in Christianity. For, as he says, 'if Christianity be an universal religion, suited not to one locality or period, but to all times and places, *it cannot but vary in its relations and dealings towards the world around it*, that is, it will develop.'[1] Moreover, great ideas, many-sided truths are not grasped all at once on their first introduction or discovery. As men seek to apprehend them—a process which in itself takes time—they find a succession of formulations each more adequate and exact than its predecessor. Misapprehensions and interpretations which exaggerate this aspect or that require correction, and we may anticipate the development of Christian doctrine as the necessary consequence. 'The method of revelation observed in Scripture abundantly confirms this anticipation.'[2] 'The whole Bible, not its prophetical portions only, is written on the principle of development.'[3] Loisy seems to have thought that Newman had not had his attention drawn to the application of the idea of evolution to the biblical revelation in the two Testaments,[4] but Newman was aware of the relevance of the principle of development to the faith of the Scriptures as paragraphs in the *Essay* make clear. Actually Newman later set out to trace the development of religion in the history of the Chosen People, as part of some Prolegomena which were to serve as an introduction to a new translation of the Scriptures. The translation was never completed and the Prolegomena were never published, because the ecclesiastical authorities discouraged the project.[5] It is true that Newman never grappled with the problems pre-

---

[1] *Essay*, p. 96 (italics mine).   [2] Ibid. p. 102.
[3] Ibid. p. 103.   [4] *Mémoires*, I, 451.
[5] *Life of Newman*, by Wilfrid Ward, I, 425 f.

sented by the literary and historical study of the Scriptures, and as Loisy says, his ideas on such subjects as the original purpose of sacrifices, the interconnection of the two Testaments, the nature of prophecy, were those of a theologian of the old school rather than of a critical well-informed historian.[1] Nevertheless, Newman's influence might have familiarised many with the idea of progressive revelation, and we may legitimately regret the caution of his ecclesiastical superiors.

Having recognised the inevitability of development Newman points out that we cannot halt the process at any particular point, e.g. Nicaea or Chalcedon. He thus rejected the High Anglican appeal to the seven Œcumenical Councils as constituting an adequate final standard. The development of doctrine inevitably continues.

The section that follows, 'On the probability of a developing authority in Christianity', is less valuable than its immediate predecessor as a contribution to the elucidation of a fundamental historical problem and more important for the light it throws on Newman's own religious outlook and for its bearing on the believer's problem. Maurice regards it as the most important section of the *Essay*. The term 'developing authority' is unsatisfactory, for the authority which Newman sought is not one that develops but one that tests developments and decides which are true and which false. The existence of such an authority is probable only if either the tests of development are inadequate for their purpose or the average believer is incapable of applying them. Both these conditions may be fulfilled and lend support to Newman's argument. His belief in the probability of the

[1] *Mémoires*, loc. cit.

53

existence in Christianity of a permanent infallible authority to maintain the essential truth of the original revelation and to ensure the right development of its doctrinal interpretation was further confirmed by his conception of the nature of religion and by his view of the need of the age in which he lived. As to the first Newman tells us that—

as the essence of all religion is authority and obedience, so the distinction between natural religion and revealed lies in this, that the one has a subjective authority, and the other an objective. Revelation consists in the manifestation of the Invisible Divine Power, or in the substitution of the voice of a Lawgiver for the voice of conscience. The supremacy of conscience is the essence of natural religion: the supremacy of Apostle or Pope or Church or Bishop is the essence of revealed: and when such external authority is taken away, the mind falls back again upon that inward guide which it possessed even before Revelation was vouchsafed.[1]

With regard to the need of his time—a need which has since intensified—Newman viewed it thus.

If the very claim to infallible arbitration in religious disputes is of so weighty importance and interest in all ages of the world, much more is it welcome at a time like the present, when the human intellect is so busy and thought so fertile and opinion so infinitely divided. The absolute need of a spiritual supremacy is at present the strongest of arguments in favour of its supply. Surely, either an objective revelation has not been given or it has been provided with means for impressing its objectiveness on the world.[2]

---

[1] *Essay on Development*, p. 124.

[2] Ibid. p. 127. Compare with this earlier treatment of this theme, the still more impressive paragraphs in the *Apologia* (pp. 269–71; Pocket edition, 1907).

Having established the probability both of developments of doctrine and of an infallible authority to test them, Newman outlines the general form of the argument in favour of regarding the Catholic developments as the true legitimate ones. The development of doctrine within the Roman Catholic communion is distinguished by consistency, permanence and the claim to infallible authority. No rival *system* can be discerned anywhere. The history of Protestantism is the history of successive reductions of a system which is confessed on all hands to bear a character of integrity and indivisibility upon it. 'Luther did but a part of the work, Calvin another portion, Socinus finished it.'[1] As to the nature of the argument in favour of the Catholic developments Newman writes wholly in the spirit of Butler's *Analogy*. We have to start from affirmations and seek to confirm them by estimates of probabilities. While admitting the danger of special pleading, Newman contended that the earlier evidence is rightly interpreted in the light of the development and should be handled so as to justify those developments. This method of enquiry is a matter of delicate and difficult discrimination. It is obviously liable to be abused and yet it is indispensable. By way of illustration, Newman cites Bishop Bull's *Defence of the Creed of Nicaea*. He thinks Bull was justified in maintaining that 'the Nicene Creed is a *natural key* for interpreting the body of Ante-Nicene theology'.[2]

The remainder of the *Essay* is devoted to illustrations of the applications of the seven tests, particularly of the first test, the preservation of the Type or Idea. In this connection Newman worked out his brilliant historical sketches, establishing the parallel between the present position of

[1] *Essay on Development*, p. 137.   [2] Ibid. p. 158.

the Roman Church and the Catholic Church in the second century, in the fourth century, and in the fifth and sixth centuries. The Roman world regarded the nascent Christian Church with exactly the same aversion, prejudice, and hostility with which the modern world regards the Roman Church. That is to say, that judged by external observers the Roman Church would appear to be identical and continuous with the primitive Church. In the fourth century, the Ancient Catholic Church contrasts with heresies and schisms very much as Rome contrasts with Protestant sects to-day. The Anglicans seemed to Newman to be in the position of the Donatists—a parallel which an article by Wiseman in the *Dublin Review* had forced on his attention. The possession of a ministry in the Apostolic succession did not save the Donatists from schism. 'If unity lies in the Apostolic succession, an act of schism is from the nature of the case impossible, for as no one can reverse his parentage, so no Church can undo the fact that its clergy have come by lineal descent from the Apostles. Either there is no such sin as schism or unity does not lie in the Episcopal form or in Episcopal ordination.' The Donatists were condemned because by no stretch of the imagination could they be regarded as the Church universal and they had repudiated communion with the Church which could make the claim to universality. 'Securus judicat orbis Terrarum.' Rome and not Canterbury represents and continues the Catholic Church of the fourth century.

The parallel between the position of the Roman Church of to-day and its position in the fifth and sixth centuries is easily established. The Tome of Leo settled the Christological question at the Council of Chalcedon. 'Roma locuta est: causa finita est.' Newman enforced the parallel in a paragraph of great rhetorical power.

If then there is now a form of Christianity such, that it extends throughout the world, though with varying measures of prominence or prosperity in separate places;—that it lies under the power of sovereigns and magistrates, in different ways alien to its faith:—that flourishing nations and great empires, professing or tolerating the Christian name, lie over against it as antagonists; that schools of philosophy and learning are supporting theories, and following out conclusions, hostile to it, and establishing an exegetical system subversive of its Scriptures;—that it has lost whole Churches by schism, and is now opposed by powerful communions once part of itself;—that it has been altogether or almost driven from some countries;—that in others its line of teachers is overlaid, its flocks oppressed, its churches occupied, its property held by what may be called a duplicate succession;—that in others its members are degenerate, and corrupt, and surpassed in conscientiousness and in virtue, as in gifts of intellect, by the very heretics whom it condemns;—that heresies are rife and bishops negligent within its own pale;—and that amid its disorders and fears there is but one voice for whose decisions its people wait with trust, one Name and one See to which they look with hope, and that name Peter and that See Rome; —such a religion is not unlike the Christianity of the fifth and sixth centuries.[1]

The discussion of the second test of fidelity of development, namely, Continuity of Principles, contains points of great importance. Here Newman asserts the enduring value of the mystical sense which the Fathers found in Scripture by means of allegorical interpretation, and which Keble discussed at length in Tract 89. 'It may almost be laid down as an historical fact that the mystical

---

[1] *Essay on Development*, p. 324.

interpretation and orthodoxy will stand or fall together.'
'The use of Scripture then, especially its spiritual or
second sense, as a medium of thought and deduction, is a
characteristic principle of the development of doctrine in
the Church.'[1] Newman had no real appreciation of the
school of Antioch whose exegesis was more scientific,
more scholarly, more honest, and less fanciful than that
of the school of Alexandria. The Reformers reverted to
Antioch, and Newman cites a passage from Hales's
Golden Remains, which sets forth admirably the principles
of sound exegesis but which Newman does not attempt
to answer because he is so convinced that the mystical
interpretation is essential to orthodoxy. The next principle
to which the Catholic developments have been con-
tinuously loyal is the assertion of the supremacy of faith
over reason. The principle is defined as follows: 'that
belief is in itself better than non-belief; that it is safer to
believe; that we must begin with believing, and that conviction will follow; that as for the reasons of believing,
they are for the most part implicit and but slightly
recognised by the mind that is under their influence;
that they consist moreover rather of presumptions and
guesses, ventures after the truth than of accurate proofs;
and that probable arguments are sufficient for conclusions
which we even embrace as most certain and turn to the
most important uses.'[2] The heretical principle is 'to
prefer Reason to Faith and to hold that things must be
considered true only in so far as they are proved'.[3] This
attempt to identify heresy with the principle of preferring
Reason to Faith (John Locke playing the part of arch-
heretic!) is singularly unfortunate. Heterodoxy as well as

---

[1] *Essay on Development*, p. 327.   [2] Ibid. p. 327.
[3] Ibid. p. 328.

orthodoxy has often asserted the Supremacy of Faith and also sought support in the mystical sense of Scripture. But Newman's summary of what he understands by the Supremacy of Faith is of great interest. It contains the germ of the *Grammar of Assent*. Beyond the mystical sense of Scripture and the supremacy of faith, Newman regards the maintenance of the dogmatic and sacramental principle as of supreme importance. On them has depended the formation of a theology.

The illustrations of the applications of the other tests do not call for extended comment. All Newman's main positions are contained in the sections already analysed.

The *Essay on Development* was a challenge to Newman's friends and disciples. They had either to follow him or re-think and re-state their positions. Those who were not so close to him could not be indifferent to Newman's apologia for his conversion. The flood of critical examinations which followed showed how deeply the publication of the *Essay* had stirred the theological waters. Two contemporary contributions stand out as still thought-provoking, one by a friend and disciple who could not continue to follow Newman, and the other by a religious leader who was never disposed to fall into step with Newman though anxious to do justice to him and his school. The first was J. B. Mozley's book, *The Theory of Development*, a critical estimate of the argumentative logical aspect of Newman's *Essay*. It appeared in substance in the *Christian Remembrancer* for January 1847. The second was 'A Review of Mr. Newman's Theory of Development' which formed the preface to Maurice's Warburton lectures on the Epistle to the Hebrews, published early in 1846. The preface is longer than the lectures. It analyses and examines Newman's *Essay* from the historical as well as the logical side. Mozley is concerned to show that the Anglican Via Media is still tenable and indeed necessary. Maurice endeavours to prove that his principles and convictions offer a better solution to Newman's problem than that which Newman accepted. Together the two books contain the best contemporary criticisms of Newman's *Essay*, being at once searching and sympathetic.

Maurice recognises both the fact of development and the problem which the apparent variation and growth of doctrine presents to us when we would consult history for the true idea of Christianity. He agrees with Newman that we cannot brush on one side the history of Christianity and form a Christianity from the Bible only as Protestants tend to do. The Vincentian canon which would find the true idea of Christianity in that which has been held true by all Christians everywhere and at all times, is no adequate guide to the perplexed enquirer. The theory, once popular with Roman theologians, of a Disciplina Arcani, which assumes that the doctrines of the Church were really in it from the first but are publicly proclaimed at the time judged appropriate by infallible authority committed to the Church, is also unsatisfying. It does not account for the process of variation and growth which leads to the development of doctrine. Maurice admits 'that neither the dictum of Vincentius, nor the theory of oriental corruptions nor the Disciplina Arcani, is adequate to solve the problems which present themselves to us in the history of Christianity'. 'I do not complain of (Mr Newman) for attempting to meet a difficulty which really exists: I am glad that he has attempted it. He has a right to require that those who oppose him should offer their own explanation, not merely raise objections to his.

The tendency characteristic of Protestantism a century ago to regard the whole history of Christianity from the close of the first to the beginning of the sixteenth century as a record of corruption best forgotten, Maurice knew to be quite indefensible. The charge against Protestants of not looking fairly at history is to a great extent true, 'and it is much better when we acknowledge a fault which we wish to see amended, not to waste time in urging exceptions or putting in pleas of mitigation'.[1] As to the medieval period in particular, 'we (Protestants) are worthily punished for our dishonesty in not doing justice to what was right and holy and noble in those ages'.[2] But Newman was mistaken in supposing that this failure to look fairly at history is either inseparable from Protestantism or peculiar to it. Mr Ward, in the *British Critic*, noted that 'the mind of Aquinas, richly as it was endowed with all manner of stores had certainly not received an historical cultivation'. Indeed, part of the attraction of the Bible for the Reformers lay in its character as an historical book. It is 'a book of life and deeds and as such, a witness against the formal divinity of the schools'. The Protestant feeling of reverence for the Bible was connected with a craving for history. Newman and the Tractarians had been too absorbed in the Fathers and the Ancient Catholic Church. They overvalued the Fathers. 'The Reformers did see some things which their predecessors did not.' Maurice took Newman severely to task for his judgments on Lutheranism. 'Mr Newman speaks often of Germany: once he says, "Lutheranism, as is well known, has by this time become simple heresy or infidelity." This fact is not well known.

---

[1] *Lectures on the Epistle to the Hebrews*, p. vi.
[2] Ibid. p. lxv.

Mr Newman does not know it himself; if he believes that Dr Pusey's work on Germany was the work of an honest eye-witness, he knows the contrary.' Protestants have no monopoly of the fault of not looking fairly at history.

Both Maurice and Mozley criticise Newman for not determining what the original seed or idea of Christianity really was. The absence of any definition vitiates the application of his Test, the Preservation of the Idea. If we do not know independently of the development what the Idea is, how can we tell whether any particular development preserves or fails to preserve the Idea? On the other hand, if as Newman seems to contend, we can only determine the nature of the Idea in the light of its developments, how can we escape the modernist conclusion that Christianity is whatever it becomes? In that case no development whatever can be dismissed as a corruption. 'Mr Newman confesses that the knowledge of the essential idea, the type of Christianity, is necessary or at all events would be most convenient, for the purpose of studying the actual history of Christianity. He confesses also that he cannot arrive at this type or leading idea, except by looking at those very developments, the soundness and faithfulness of which are to be ascertained by help of it. The further we advance in the book, the more continually will this strange contradiction be forcing itself upon our notice.'[1]

There is a serious ambiguity in Newman's use of the term 'idea' of which Newman himself hardly seems to have been aware. He has defined ideas as habitual judgments which will be real if they correspond with something external, and fictitious if no object is represented by them. But when he speaks of the Preservation

[1] *Lectures on Hebrews*, p. xxi.

of the Type or Idea of Christianity he must mean or should mean, not the habitual judgments in the minds of Christian men, but the essential objective reality to which these judgments are related. When he writes, 'The Scriptures were intended to create an idea, and that idea is not in the sacred text, but in the mind of the reader', obviously the idea, the habitual judgment created in the mind of the reader is not the same as the idea or type or essence of Christianity, the preservation of which is the first test of all developments. The Scriptures could not create ideas in the former sense if they did not contain the idea in the latter sense. 'The reverent reader of Scripture, be he Romanist or Protestant, does think that the idea which he receives from Scripture is not merely in his mind; that it is also in the text.' It is difficult to see in what sense we can regard the Scriptures as containing a revelation, if they do not suffice to determine for us the primary idea, the type of Christianity. Maurice is prepared to follow Newman in discussing antecedent probabilities and he asks whether 'there be not an antecedent probability that the Scriptures would unfold that primary idea which he, Newman, needs and yet denounces men for venturing to seek; that it would explain that law or method of development which, he says, it exhibits so remarkably; and so that it would save us from the monstrous contradiction of looking into the history itself for that with which it is to be compared, and by which it is to be judged'.[1]

Another antecedent probability, deduced from what we know of Scripture and history, is that when 'large developments do exist as matters of fact' some of these will be corruptions or fleshly developments. J. B. Mozley

[1] Ibid. p. xxvi.

brought out this point more forcibly than Maurice when he insisted that corruption may be due to exaggeration as well as to defect. The possibility of exaggerated development was admitted, but its existence in fact was not recognised in Newman's argument. None of his tests would detect corruption by excess. It is easy to see from this legitimate observation how Mozley could continue to hold to the Anglican Via Media.

Maurice might have said that none of the Tests except the first, the Preservation of the Idea, would detect corruption by excess. But as we have seen Newman had rendered the first Test inapplicable by confusing idea as opinion or judgment with idea as type or essence. The whole force of Maurice's detailed arguments depends on his fundamental difference from Newman on the vital importance of the first test and the possibility of applying it. He differed from Newman on the character of the revelation in the Scriptures, on the nature of authority, on the function of the Church, on the place of dogma and doctrine in the life of the Church.

The further analysis of Maurice's critique of Newman's Essay may start from his examination of Newman's exposition of the dogmatic principle.

That opinions in religion are not matters of indifference but have a definite bearing on the position of their holders in the Divine Sight, is a principle on which the Evangelical Faith has from the first developed and on which that Faith has been the first to develop. I suppose it hardly had any exercise under the Law; the zeal and obedience of the ancient people being employed in the maintenance of divine worship and the overthrow of idolatry, not in assertion of opinion. Faith is in this, as in other respects, a characteristic of the Gospel, except in so far as it was anticipated as its time drew near....The Greek Philosophers...did not commonly attach sanctity or reality to opinions, or view them in a religious light. Our Saviour was the first to 'bear witness to the Truth' and to die for it, when 'before Pontius Pilate he witnessed a good confession'.[1]

In this passage Newman gives unguarded expression to his conviction that dogma is essential to religion, that orthodoxy, the holding of correct opinions, is a matter of first importance. To many this will seem to be characteristic not of the Evangelical Faith from the first but of the Evangelical Faith as modified and interpreted by the Greek spirit. Opinions in religion were no matters of indifference to Maurice but he could not attach such exaggerated importance to dogma. He legitimately noted 'the startling admission which Mr Newman makes,' that 'Christianity—just so far as it is dogmatic, is a departure from the principle and Type which are given us in the Old Testament. Elijah testified, as Mr Newman says, against idolatry—as he himself says—"That the Lord was God." Christians have a work different in kind from this, to testify in favour of certain opinions.'[2] A distinction so strange must lead us to suspect that there is some radical error in Newman's argument. Can he seriously suggest that when our Lord said 'I came to bear witness to the Truth', He meant 'I came to bear witness to certain opinions'? The suggestion has only to be formulated to be dismissed. Elijah bare witness for the living God—for Him who was and who is and who is to come. Mr Newman says he did not bear witness for opinions. But he *did* bear witness for the Truth, for that which actually is. Our Lord said, "I came into the world to bear witness for the Truth", but He had said before, "I am the Truth."

[1] *Essay*, p. 339.   [2] *Lectures*, p. xc.

What were all His discourses with the Jews but so man'
witnesses of this?'[1] The Truth is embodied not in a set o
opinions but in a person.

Inevitably Maurice was dissatisfied with Newman'
account of the supremacy of faith. If faith means, as i
seems to do in some passages in the *Essay*, the acceptanc
of opinions or trust in conclusions deduced from probabl
arguments, then it can hardly be opposed to reason o
superior to it. But if we may judge by the Apostle'
Creed, the primitive faith centred on a person. 'Th
"believe" is really lost in Him who is believed. Th
Faith goes out of the *I* into the object.' Actually, Luthe
asserts the supremacy of faith as trust in a person mor
forcibly than the Scholastics.

Luther...cuts through (scholastic) questions...by callin
upon men to believe in a Person. Faith is everything wit
him; he will not hear of reason. The last is for schoolmer
the first for poor sinners. But faith is always connected in h
mind with a Gospel. Good news of Christ the Son of God an
the Son of Man, the Deliverer, are preached to men; the
believe and are blessed. By and by the Gospel ceases to 1
the proclamation of Christ; only the proclamation of certai
doctrines concerning Him or of certain results from these doc
trines. Faith is demanded for these. Controversies aris
concerning them, and the intellect...claims its share i
judging concerning them, in rejecting them.[2]

Faith as trust in Christ and faith as the acceptance
certain doctrines concerning Him cannot be simpl
equated, however closely they may be connected. Th
distinction is apparent in the New Testament in th
difference in the case of the word 'Faith' in St Paul

---

[1] *Lectures on Hebrews*, p. xci.   [2] Ibid. p. lxxxiii.

arlier Epistles and in the Pastorals.[1] A little later on, Ritschl was to press home the same distinction on hard-shell Lutheran orthodoxy. Maurice was justified in asserting that the supremacy of faith was not a principle which distinguished Catholicism from Protestantism and that in Catholicism the primitive Evangelical faith was too readily identified with the acceptance of notions or opinions through overemphasis on the dogmatic principle.

The revelation contained in the Scriptures is doubtless subject to development. This is plainly asserted in the opening verse of the letter to the Hebrews, and it is in-volved in the very conception of two Testaments or Covenants. The nature of the revelation is the disclosure of God's will and purpose in events, in His mighty acts, culminating in the coming of Christ. The Scriptures must not be treated as 'a collection of notions or opinions about certain great subjects' which can be systematised into a theology. They are the record of God's dealings with our race, whereby we come to understand our rela-tion to our fellow man and our relation to God. And the unity of the Scriptures is in Christ. 'The history of the world requires a Bible to interpret it.... The Bible we have will fulfil this office provided it be a Bible; that is, provided the old notion of its being a whole is not a fiction; that it is a whole because it is the record of the historical method by which it pleased God that His Son should be manifested to man.'[2] Those who look upon Christ as the subject of Scripture can learn and should learn from the Fathers, the Schoolmen, the Mystics, the Reformers. 'Only they do not refuse further to be taught of God by the experience of individual life, by the actual history of the world, how to receive the witness of His

[1] Cf. Gal. ii. 20 with I Tim. iii. 13.   [2] *Lectures on Hebrews*, p. lxxix.

word more directly, to darken it less by shadows ca
from their own minds, to make it less a matter of priva
interpretation, to tremble more lest what is meant t
explain the ways of God to man, should, through or
fault or conceit, perplex them more.'[1] 'If they cann
deny that the Bible teaches them to understand Fathe
and Schoolmen and Reformers more than these hel
them to understand the Bible, that on the whole the te
seems to them brighter and clearer than the commen
this does not prove that they delight less in the landscap
which the sun brings out before them or that there is
single rivulet or hedgerow in it which they would n
willingly be acquainted with.'[2] In short, all things ar
ours, if we are Christ's.

It seemed to Maurice that any one who appreciated th
revelation in the Scriptures would seek for a catholi
Church and not for a catholic system. Newman, on th
other hand, was attracted to Catholicism as a systen
No rival system has appeared. Consistency is one of th
charms of Romanism. In Maurice's eyes, this was defec
A church committed to a system cannot be genuine
catholic, even if the label be attached to the system.
catholic system is a contradiction in terms.

A passage quoted from Guizot by Mr Newman respectir
the 'harmonious development of Romanism' and the contr
dictions of the Reformers is most instructive. Romanis
persecute, Protestants persecute. The Romanist feels that he
consistent, the Protestant feels that he is inconsistent. Henc
the first has a strength and justification in his course whic
the second cannot have. So it is in the whole formation
their systems. The Romanist's is round and smooth, th
Protestant's irregular, jagged, broken. Evidently the one is

[1] *Lectures on Hebrews*, p. lxxix.   [2] Ibid. p. lxxx.

aster of his art, the other is a blunderer, knows very little
out it, yet will be continually making the attempt....Each
w attempt at the creation of a system leads to new divisions
d parties. A disheartening result indeed...if, without
system, we can have no religion, no theological science, no
hurch. But if religious feeling, exercises, life have been
amped and destroyed by the bondage of system; if system
every department has been the plague of science, making it,
t the knowledge of that which is, but merely the aggregate
human conceptions; if therefore it has been especially the
rse of theological science, which is grounded on the Revela-
n of Him who is and was and is to come, and which should
ever exhibiting His revealed Name in some new aspects,
interpreting some new aspect in human history; if, lastly,
system in all ages has been hiding the Church from view,
aking it assume the character of a school or sect, destroying
reality, robbing it of its Centre—then thanks be to God that
are reminded by so many proofs how vain it is for us to
uld a system, call it Protestant, Anglican, Catholic, what
u like.[1]

We may note in this connection how clearly Tennyson's
rse echoes Maurice's conviction:

> Our little systems have their day,
>   They have their day and cease to be:
>   They are but broken lights of Thee,
> And Thou, O Christ, art more than they.

'The Bible sets forth God as actually speaking to men,
actually ruling in the midst of them.' The Kingdom of
hrist is a present Kingdom. If the essence of religion
authority and obedience, the authority is always the
thority of God in Christ and the obedience is always
e conscientious and reasonable obedience of free men.

[1] Ibid. pp. cxxi, cxxii.

This is the meaning of the new covenant. 'They sha
teach no more every man his neighbour and every ma
his brother, saying, Know the Lord: for they shall a
know me, from the least of them to the greatest c
them, saith the Lord.' Newman's suggestion that cor
science is the supreme authority in natural religior
while revealed religion substitutes the voice of
Lawgiver for the voice of conscience, is quite untenabl
As Martineau claimed, conscience is the *seat* of auth
rity, but never its source. And conscience remair
the seat of authority, by whatever medium the wor
of God is made known to it. The Lawgiver is alway
God himself, and He does not commit His authority t
Apostle or Pope or Church or Bishop, though all thes
may be His instruments and witnesses. 'All orders of me
are appointed by Him and are ruling under Him.' 'Ju
so far as they know this and live and act in the faith of i
they are doing their right work in the world, are helpin
to expound the laws and principles of the Divine Goverr
ment, are helping to bring man into that service which :
freedom. And just so far as they are not doing this, bt
are setting up their own power and authority and ar
working as parts of a system instead of working as servan
of the living God, just so far are they false kings, and fals
priests, and false prophets.' As Rendel Harris used to say
God has not served the infallibility out yet: He has kept
to Himself. Newman assumed that all would admit th
infallibility of the Apostles, and the assumption woul
have been granted by most Protestants when he wrot
The concession would not be made easily to-day
Maurice agreed that the Church to-day should have th
same authoritative guidance as the primitive Churc
had. But that guidance did not derive from some ir

fallible authority committed to the Apostles and no such authority is committed to the Church now. The objectiveness of the revelation is impressed on the world, not by the provision of a developing authority, but by the historicity of Jesus, by the continuing presence of His spirit in the whole Christian fellowship, and by the judgments of God in history. 'Often times it would not be so much by the agency of men as by fearful historical crises, that He would make His purposes evident and confound the counterfeits of them.'[1] To Maurice, twelve centuries of Mahometan domination in the near east seemed indicative of a divine judgment on some features of the Christianity both of the Roman and the Orthodox Churches.

Though Maurice dissented vigorously from Newman's conclusions, he had no doubt as to the seriousness of Newman's arguments and never for a moment questioned Newman's sincerity. Candid minds are not likely to revive prejudices and misunderstandings which were answered once for all in the *Apologia*. But Maurice's wise observations are worth recalling, because similar unjust suspicions may attach to similar conversions whether religious or political. Maurice wrote:

It seems to me that widely as Mr Newman's present conclusions are distinct from those he once adopted, he has not arrived at them by any tortuous or illegitimate process.... Nor am I much influenced by documents which have been brought forward to prove that Mr Newman was in heart feeling a Romanist while he adhered to our Communion. *Chronology in the history of mental conflicts is most uncertain* : to-day there may be sensations of vehement disgust for that which was once very dear, to-morrow a return to first love. If th

---

[1] *Lectures on Hebrews*, p. xl.

decision is ultimately an honest one, we have no right to assume a cognizance of previous struggles and revulsions of feeling, which are really known only to the Judge of all.[1]

Maurice appreciated fairly the development of Newman's thought. From 1833 on, Newman had felt called to stem the tide of Liberalism or Rationalism. He had sought barriers against it, in reaffirming the Apostolic succession and authority of the ministry, by reviving interest in the Fathers, and by deepening reverence for the Sacraments.

He finds the barriers he thought would preserve us from Rationalism insufficient. Is he not right? Are they not insufficient? Will Sacraments avail, if we look at them apart from Him, if they do not testify of His presence? The Rationalist has gone beyond all visible things and has asked what is at the ground of them. If we can, in deepest awe, but also with calmness and certainty, give answer, all forms and orders and visible things will repeat it. We shall see them in a new light; they will have a new meaning for us. We shall satisfy, not stifle, the questionings of others; our own ground will be what it has ever been, but we shall *know* that we are standing on the Rock of Ages.[2]

For all their differences, Maurice and Newman had much in common. They were united in giving 'praise to the Holiest in the height!'

[1] *Lectures on Hebrews,* p. cxxviii.   [2] Ibid. p. cxxviii.

CHAPTER IV

CHRISTIANITY AND THE
RELIGIONS OF THE WORLD

❧━━━❧

IN 1845 and 1846 Maurice delivered two sets of four lectures each on the foundation of Robert Boyle, known to history as the father of modern chemistry and the uncle of the Earl of Cork! The first series described the leading religions of the world and the second dealt with the relation of Christianity to them. Published in book form, the lectures won considerable popularity. They have the merit of entire freedom from the old theological tone of bullying.

Let me supplement this inadequate appreciation by citing the warm tribute paid to the book by F. J. Powicke, in the article previously cited. Maurice's Boyle Lecture, 'The Religions of the World',

turned out to be, perhaps, the most popular of all his writings, and, if my own case could indicate the reason why, it was because the book delivered people from a spiritual nightmare. I can well remember the horror with which as a boy I listened to a preacher who besought his hearers to support foreign missions because, apart from the Gospel with its plan of salvation, there was no hope of escape for the heathen from everlasting punishment.... The matter haunted me for years, and bred doubts which threw scorn on talk about the love of God. Maurice's book scattered them like the dawn. It was glorious to be shown on the best of evidence, the teaching of the New Testament, that God is the loving Father of all men, that He has never left Himself without a witness to them and in them, that the Eternal Word has ever been the inner light of every man—the hidden source of all the goodness and truth to which any man has ever attained: that the Word became flesh and dwelt among us full of grace and truth on purpose to reveal this fact, and claim all men as His brothers, and offer Himself to them as the fulfiller of all their dreams of deliverance from error and sin, and open the way for them to the Father, and assure them of a love which takes note of every human soul, judges every human soul fairly and mercifully, and is bent upon the redemption of every human soul both now and always.

After this lucid summary of Maurice's teaching, Dr Powicke adds, 'Am I wrong in thinking that this Boyle Lecture...did more than anything else to inspire that new attitude toward the non-Christian world which is now [1930] characteristic of the missionary and those who send him forth?'[1]

Leslie Stephen, while recognizing the presence of this honourable characteristic, thinks Maurice attempted too much. 'He was venturing somewhat beyond his depth in discussing so wide a subject.' It must be confessed that a discussion of Hinduism which contains no reference to Karma and re-incarnation, and which does not distinguish clearly the three modes of salvation recognised in Hinduism, leaves much to be desired. Similarly, a treatment of Buddhism which says nothing of the four noble truths or the noble eight-fold path can hardly be regarded as adequate. It is a pioneer work and even of the information at his disposal Maurice did not always make the best use.

Leslie Stephen detected in the book the constant use of a curious tense which he happily described as the con-

[1] *Congregational Quarterly*, April 1930, p. 179.

jectural preterite. Maurice frequently asserts that Moslem Hindu or Buddhist will have thought this or that, or must have meant this, that, and the other. The conjectural preterite is certainly a dangerous toy, but it covers two very different processes. It may present us either with flashes of genuine intuitive insight or with an a priori misreading of the evidence. Maurice will furnish us with instances of both kinds. Leslie Stephen suspected him of reading himself into other minds all the time, turning other people into Mauriceians. He does do this on occasion, but there is much sympathetic understanding in his conjectures as to what has gone on in the minds of men of past generations and of other faiths.

In the introduction to his first course, Maurice notes a change in men's attitude towards religion as a result of their experience in the French Revolution. In the 1840's, men were beginning to be convinced,

that if Religion had had only the devices and tricks of statesmen or priests to rest upon, it could not have stood at all; for that these are very weak things indeed, which, when they are left to themselves, a popular tempest must carry utterly away. If they have lasted a single day, it must have been because they had something better, truer than themselves to sustain them. This better, truer thing, it seems to be allowed, must be that very faith in men's hearts upon which so many disparaging epithets were cast, and which it was supposed could produce no fruits that were not evil and hurtful.

The same lesson seems to be emerging from the continuance and revival of religion in Russia. Religion is not just the opiate of the people or a defensive weapon in the armoury of capitalism. Perhaps even more impressive is the war against Hitlerism on what is rightly called the Eternal Front. Karl Barth did not claim too much for the stand of the Confessional Church in Germany when he spoke of it as a small proof of the reality of faith. Faith is a real power, and faith is not dead yet.

It may, however, be questioned whether the vitality of religion is proof of anything beyond the continued presence of faith in human hearts. Hope springs eternal. Is there anything more to it than that? And so long as men believe in something beyond themselves, does anything else matter? Are not specific theologies just the embodiments of men's intense deep-seated aspirations? As Maurice puts it,

> But then, it is asked, is there not ground for supposing that all the different religious systems, and not one only, may be legitimate products of that faith which is so essential a part of men's constitution? Are not they manifestly adapted to peculiar times and localities and races? Is it not probable that the theology of all alike is something merely accidental, an imperfect theory about our relations to the universe, which will in due time give place to some other? Have we not reason to suppose that Christianity, instead of being, as we have been taught, a Revelation, has its root in the heart and intellect of man, as much as any other system?

The Theosophists are always with us to assure us that all religions mean the same thing in the end. But Maurice was concerned with a more radical scepticism—to wit, the tendency to look on all theology as having its origin in the spiritual nature and faculties of man. Thus, Lowes Dickinson regarded theologies as conjectural helpful mythologies which faith constructs to satisfy the incurably religious nature of man. Dr Julian Huxley's *Religion without Revelation* reflects the same attitude. Man's sense of the sacred generates his religious beliefs, but these beliefs do not find support in objective reality.

Maurice does not meet this position by the old assumption that one religion must be true, and all others false, nor does he adopt exactly Dr Kraemer's distinction between religions which embody men's religious reactions to nature, and religions of revelation.[1] He claimed that there is some truth, but not the same truth, in every religion, and that whatever truth they exhibit must come from the source of all truth. He asserts that discovery and revelation are more nearly synonymous words than any we can find in our language, and like Justin Martyr, he claims that Greek philosophers such as Socrates were divinely guided. But in the end, he agrees in advance with Dr Kraemer inasmuch as he sees in Judaism, Christianity and Islam an assertion of the divine initiative which is lacking in other religions. These three are religions of revelation in a deeper sense than others. Commenting on the theory of religion without revelation, which is still popular with Julian Huxley, Maurice asked 'Is it the adequate explanation of *any* system? Do not *all* demand another ground than the human one? Is not Christianity the consistent assertor of that higher ground? Does it not distinctly and consistently refer every human feeling and consciousness to that ground? Is it not *for this reason* able to interpret and reconcile the other religions of the earth? Does it not in this way prove itself to be *not* a human system, but *the* Revelation, which human beings require?'

His task then, as Maurice conceived it, is to discover the elements of truth in other religions, to show how Christianity, rightly understood, can do justice to them, to admit that in actual fact Christianity has needed the corrective contained in the insights of other faiths, to

[1] See *The Christian Message in a non-Christian World.*

77

suggest that Christianity, again rightly understood, can supply what is lacking in other faiths. Throughout he has in mind the theory that the religions of the world are but so many products of man's wishful thinking, and also that kind of speculation about religions which blurs all the distinctions between them and so misses their true significance.

He starts with Islam. Carlyle had already challenged the conventional estimate of Mahomet as an impostor—an estimate which finds lyrical expression in one of the hymns for the use of the people called Methodists. It is so representative of the older Evangelical view of the prophet of Arabia that I cannot forbear quoting it.

> Sun of unclouded Righteousness,
>   With healing in thy wings arise,
> A sad benighted world to bless,
>   Which now in sin and error lies,
> Wrapt in Egyptian night profound;
> With chains of hellish darkness bound.
>
> The smoke of the infernal cave,
>   Which half the Christian world o'erspread,
> Disperse, thou heavenly Light, and save
>   The souls by that Impostor led,
> That Arab-thief, as Satan bold,
> Who quite destroy'd thy Asian fold.
>
> O might the blood of sprinkling cry
>   For those who spurn the sprinkled blood!
> Assert thy glorious Deity,
>   Stretch out thine arm, thou triune God!
> The Unitarian fiend expel,
> And chase his doctrine back to hell.

Maurice actually heard Carlyle's lecture on Mahomet, in 1840, and he penned this interesting comment on it in a letter to his wife:

...The lecture was by far the most animated and vehement I ever heard from him. It was a passionate defence of Mahomet from all the charges that have been brought against him, and a general panegyric upon him and his doctrine. He did not bring out any new maxims, but it was a much clearer and more emphatic commentary than the former lecture upon his two or three standing maxims: that no great man can be insincere; that a doctrine which spreads must have truth in it; and that this particular one was a vesture fitted to the time and circumstances of the common truths which belong to all religions. I felt throughout how much *more* kind and tolerant towards the truth in all forms of faith and opinion he can be, and should be who does in his heart believe Jesus Christ to be the Son of God, and that all systems are feeling after Him as the common centre of the world, than Carlyle can ever be while he regards the world as without a centre, and the doctrine of Christ's incarnation, passion, and resurrection, as only one of the mythical vestures in which certain notions which, without such a vesture, he secretly knows and confesses to be good-for-nothing abstractions, have wrapped themselves up. At the same time, the miserable vagueness into which he sometimes fell, his silly rant about the great bosom of nature, which was repeated in this lecture several times, which, as you observe, he would laugh to scorn in any other man, together with the most monstrous confusions both intellectual and moral, even while he evidently wished to assert the distinction between right and wrong, convinced me whither his tolerance would lead in any mind in which it was not corrected, as it is in his, by a real abhorrence of what is base and false, and by a recklessness of logical consistency, if so be he can bring out his different half-conceptions in some strong expressive language.[1]

He was convinced that Carlyle failed to indicate the real source of Mahomet's strength and influence. To

[1] *Life and Letters*, I, 282.

what are we to attribute the vitality of Islam? It is no doubt closely associated with conquest, but it is not to be explained by the ruthless use of arms. Carlyle is right in protesting against the supposition that the spread of Islam is the result of successful imposture. It is not to be explained either by plagiarism from the Scriptures or by gems contained in the Koran, though the Arabic of the Koran still captivates its hearers. In spite of Carlyle, hero-worship will hardly account for the vitality of Islam. A negative hatred of idolatry does not take us to the end of the matter either. The essential strength of Islam is to be found in its thought of God or rather its faith in God. It is the proclamation of the living and eternal God and a demand for submission to His will. This faith, and not the hopes of a paradise of sensual felicity, inspired the Moslem warriors. To Maurice it seemed that the conquest of Islam came as a judgment on a Christian Church which by its veneration of relics and icons was putting human mediators between the worshipper and God—a Church engaged in speculative controversies about God and Christ, and forgetful of the true nature of the realities they discussed so freely. 'Notions about God more or less occupied them: but God Himself was not in all their thoughts.' With that we might compare Dr Thomas Hodgkin's comment on the Christological controversies of the fifth century. 'As you read the records of the Robber Synod and study the polemics of Cyril of Alexandria, you exclaim, They have taken away my Lord and I know not where they have laid Him.'

Islam brings no comfort to those who seek ethics without revelation, and religion without theology.

We are told that the mere theological part of religious systems is only a loose, flimsy drapery for certain maxims of morality, or certain ideas about the nature and spiritual destinies of man. How does the study of Mahometanism bear out this opinion? Is it a collection of moral maxims which has been its strength? Is it some theory or conception about the nature of man? Precisely the opposite assertion is true. All mere maxims, all mere ideas about the nature of man, have proved weak and helpless before this proclamation of a living and Eternal God. The theological transcendent principle is just the one which has stood its ground, which has reappeared age after age, which the most ignorant warriors felt was true and mighty for them, for which no cultivation has provided any substitute.

I am inclined to think Maurice's treatment of Islam the best part of the book. He sees some of the weaknesses of the Moslem faith very clearly. It is at its best when active and aggressive. It meets men's needs in time of peace less successfully. The sovereignty of God is apt to be understood as, and to be reflected in, political despotism. Curiously enough, he does not stress the most serious defect of Islam, its attitude towards women. He sees that the contrast between Islam and Hinduism suggests the former's limitations. Islam is a religion of action, Hinduism is a religion of rest. For Islam, God is will; for Hinduism, God is intelligence. Obedience, submission in Islam are matched or contrasted with contemplation and mystical absorption in Hinduism. For the one the saint is soldier and lawgiver, for the other student and mystic. Maurice comments understandingly on the meaning of the great equation, 'That art Thou', which identifies the soul of man with the spirit of the universe. He notes also the effect of confining the realisation of this identification to the twice-born. Whether or not he was right in tracing the origin of caste to a religious difference, he was justified in his view of its religious significance. The realisation of oneness with the One is the privilege of the Brahmin caste. While this conception of ultimate reality will haunt the popular imagination and determine the underlying conception of religion, yet the thing is high, and most men cannot attain unto it. Hence the need of lesser manifestations of the deity, in Vishnu the preserver, in Siva the destroyer, in Krishna the restorer. Here, too, if Maurice thought the peoples of India first tried to live on the level of the great equation, and developed an interest in Vishnu and Siva when the more austere creed was found to be too high for them, I suspect he was mistaken. The popular devotions must have accompanied the lofty flights of Hindu religious philosophy from the beginning. Their varying intensity no doubt depends in part on the rigidity of the distinction between twice-born and once-born, and on the exclusiveness of claims made for and by the Brahmin caste. The popular devotions persist and from time to time intensify not merely because only the twice-born can enjoy the full salvation, but because the full salvation does not satisfy. The equation 'That art Thou', leaves the world itself and our life in it, an enigma, and this will never content men.

As I have already indicated, Maurice is perhaps at his weakest in his discussion of Buddhism. But he rightly saw in Buddhism a protest against the sacerdotal claims of the Brahmin caste, an assertion of a way of salvation open to all. The philosopher disengages himself from the priest and makes a more direct appeal to the common man. But Buddhism has limitations of its own, since it appears to be a monastic religion.

When in the second series of lectures Maurice turns to

consider the relation of Christianity to these different faiths, and more particularly shews what Christianity has in common with them, he is most successful in his account of the relation of Christianity to Islam and less successful in handling Hinduism and Buddhism. Judaism, Christianity and Islam are alike in insisting on God's initiative. They are alike in recognising the prophetic call of individuals, the revelation of God's will through individuals. They are alike in recognising that nations may be called to act as the instruments of God's justice. Maurice held that this can never be the highest task of the Christian nation, yet he thought it was a task which even a Christian nation might have to discharge. At the same time, he perceives the extraordinary difficulty of associating any such activity with the gospel. Commenting on the Moslem conviction that they were God's soldiers, he says,

They were sure that they had a commission from Him to punish a people the cup of whose iniquities was full. They were sure they were not doing a work for themselves, but were executing the purposes of His Will. And this the Mahometan says is the true law of armies, the right spirit for men of later as well as earlier days to fight in and act in. They must feel that an Unseen Power is in the midst of their host; that they are His soldiers. We are often told that the opinion is a mistaken and a dangerous one; one which belonged to Judaism, and which Christianity discountenances....But I do not think that any Christian nation has ever been the worse for believing that it was acting as the minister of God. Our forms and proclamations always express this. Have we been better when these forms and proclamations were real and significant, or when they were false? It seems to me, that the more we come to think these phrases not merely phrases, but the expression of what is true, the more simple and honest

our lives will be, and that when to any nation they become
mere phrases, its life, I need not say its Christianity, is gone.
I feel very sure that the sense of a Divine Presence has
never utterly forsaken, and does not forsake, any host of
Christian men fighting by land or sea; or that, if it does,
their arms become palsied, and they become the shame of
their enemies.[1]

Yet Maurice is clear that this is not the highest work of all.

But that particular work which was assigned to the Jewish
nation, of putting down wrong and violence, of asserting
justice and judgment, though it can never be obsolete, though
each nation must be called upon in its own place and circumstances to fulfil it, cannot be the highest work of all. For He
who did the highest work of all, did it by suffering, submission, sacrifice; the greatest triumph over the greatest evils
was won in this way. Power manifested itself in weakness;
He who was most meek, proved Himself to be most a King.
He who most proved Himself to be Divine, did so by becoming
one with the poorest and vilest.[2]

Another important feature of the three religions under
discussion is their reliance on the record in a book. But
the reverence for the letter which characterises the
Jew's attitude to the Torah and the Moslem's attitude
towards the Koran ought not to be the Christian's attitude
towards the Bible.

Islam has thus many features in common with Christianity, but in Maurice's judgment Mahomet was essentially
reactionary. He was asserting the kind of monotheism
which had been the starting-point of the Jewish faith.
He was asking the world to begin its history again and
to begin it with no hope of progress. Revelation ends
with the Koran. Moreover, Mahomet's conception of the

[1] *The Religions of the World*, pp. 139–40.   [2] Ibid. pp. 149–50.

unity of God is too simple and his conception of God's sovereignty too capricious for men to rest in them.

Because the Mahometan recognises a mere Will governing all things, and that Will not a loving Will, he is converted, as we saw that he had been in the course of his history, from a noble witness of a Personal Being into the worshipper of a dead necessity. Because he will not admit that there has been a Man in the world who was one with God—a Man who exercised power over nature, and yet whose main glory consisted in giving up Himself, therefore he cannot really assert the victory of man over visible things when he tries most to do so. He glorifies the might of arms when he talks of the might of submission. Because he does not acknowledge a loving Will acting upon men's wills, to humble them in themselves, and to raise them to God, therefore he becomes the enslaver of his fellows, therefore cheerful obedience to a master, which for a while distinguished him, becomes servitude to a tyrant. Because he will not acknowledge that the highest and divinest unity is that of love, but rests all upon the mere unity of sovereignty, he has never been able to establish one complete government upon the earth.

In his discussion of affinities between Christianity and the religions of India, Maurice is inclined to force his parallels. The universality asserted in Buddhism has no very close parallel in the outpouring of the Spirit upon all flesh on the day of Pentecost. There is little connection between the Hindu's claims for the twice-born and the necessity of a second birth asserted in the Fourth Gospel. The conception of Brahma as Intelligence is not very closely allied to the Logos-doctrine or to the Wisdom-doctrine that preceded the Logos-doctrine. When we come to Incarnation and sacrifice, the parallels and associations are obviously more striking. But it is just here that Maurice, rightly as it seems to me, detects the great difference.

(But) it is just in the point of deepest sympathy with this ancient people that we arrive at the secret of our opposition. Upon the question to *whom* the sacrifice should be offered, whether by it we propitiate a Siva, or surrender ourselves in faith and truth to Him who cares for us and loves us; whether it is to overcome the reluctance of an enemy, or is the offering of our own reluctant wills to a Father in the name of one who has presented and is ever presenting His own filial and complete Sacrifice—upon this issue, let us understand it well, our controversy with Hindooism turns.

All Brahminical acts, services, sacraments, imply an effort or scheme on the part of the creature to raise himself to God. All Christian acts, services, sacraments, imply that God has sought for the creature that He might raise him to Himself. The differences in our thoughts of God, of the priest, of the sacrifice, all go back to this primary difference.[1]

I hope I have carried the analysis far enough to illustrate Maurice's approach and make clear some of his main judgments. Perhaps it will suffice to enable us to estimate the justice of Leslie Stephen's criticisms. Those criticisms turn on three main points. He insists in the first place that Maurice was a mystic at bottom. 'The confusion between an emotion and a cognition runs through Mr Maurice's whole method. The mystic is conscious of a feeling of awe and calls it the perception of the presence of an indwelling power. The consciousness becomes the guarantee for the reality of its supposed object.' In the second place, it is suggested that Maurice simply interpreted other religions with his own religion as a standard. But this procedure might be adopted equally

[1] *The Religions of the World*, pp. 181–2.

well by the exponents of other faiths. 'Assuming any religion whatever for the centre of operations I may thus pronounce that the elements which other religions possess in common with it are the vital truths, and that the other elements are excrescences.' In the third place, Maurice professes to appeal to history, and loses his case on appeal. 'He is to show that history confirms the great truth, that Christ is the light of the world. Christianity is the revelation of man's true relation to his Creator and to his fellow-men. All other religions imply a dim perception of the same eternal truths. Therefore the proclamation of Christianity supplies the necessary complement to them all; clears all doubts and reduces all apparent confusion to order.' 'We have now only to appeal to history to see whether, in fact, Christianity has given this satisfaction.' Actually, we do not find Moslems, Hindoos, Buddhists, Confucians, discovering this satisfaction in Christianity. Is not the proper deduction that Christianity is, like the other religions, a product of the human mind, not a revelation from the supreme source of light and power?

Professor Laird, reviewing a new book on Schleiermacher, in *Philosophy* (November 1943, p. 271), provides illustrations of the first two points of Leslie Stephen. Commenting on Schleiermacher's 'feeling of absolute dependence,' he says, 'Some may suspect that Schleiermacher illegitimately translated the "feeling of absolute dependence" into "the feeling of dependence on the Absolute".' Leslie Stephen attributes a similar illegitimate translation to Maurice. Again Laird says, 'If as Schleiermacher seems to have thought, the Christian faith exhibits a form in which there is a plain and also a beautiful development of religious feeling, it would seem to be open to Mohammedan, Indian and Persian theologians to

say the same thing of their religions'. This is Leslie
Stephen's second contention. But there, I think, Laird
and Stephen part company; and the problems Laird
puts up to the theologian are other than those of Leslie
Stephen.

What then are we to say to these criticisms?

Whether or no Maurice confused an emotion with a
cognition, he certainly refused to separate them. The
feeling of awe is not normally aroused without the perception of an object of some kind. The idea of a pure
emotion which generates objects for its satisfaction,
belongs either to an outworn faculty psychology, or to a
Freudian theory of projection which will prove as
dangerous to science as to religion. The feeling of awe
normally involves an awareness of something which
evokes it. It does not indeed guarantee either that the
object is worthy of reverence or that it will be correctly
apprehended by the worshipper, but the object evokes
the emotion, the emotion does not create the object. It is
doubtful whether there can be any such emotion as a
feeling of absolute dependence. The feeling is either a
feeling of actual dependence on something or a longing
for something on which to depend. In the first case, it
may be rightly understood as a feeling of dependence on
the absolute. In the latter case, we must admit that the
longing may be so intense that a man will clutch at anything to satisfy it. But unless such a desire can be shown
to be morbid or unnatural, it must resemble hunger and
thirst, the innate instinctive urges on which life depends.
It is not for nothing that the Psalmist compares his
longing for God to the hart panting after cooling streams.
It is not for nothing that Jesus spoke of hungering and
thirsting after righteousness. These spiritual desires are as

intense and as natural as are physical desires, and it would be an irrational universe which denied them satisfaction. Furthermore Maurice would not confess to being a mystic in Leslie Stephen's sense. It has been suggested that 'The religions of the world can be distinguished into those which emphasise the object and those which insist on experience. For the first class, religion is an attitude of faith and conduct directed to a power without. For the second, it is an experience to which the individual attaches supreme value.' On this division, Maurice belongs to the first and the mystic of Leslie Stephen's argument to the second. Maurice did not have a feeling of awe and then look round for a historical embodiment of it or support for it. His religious consciousness did not guarantee the reality of its supposed object. The fact of Christ is given and this supreme fact determined his religious consciousness. At the same time, he believed that subconsciously or consciously man longed for such a Saviour. No doubt it is a venturesome generalisation, but when Job cried 'O that there were a daysman or an umpire between us, that he might lay his hand upon both of us!' Maurice believed he spoke for mankind. Job's conviction that his Vindicator lives and will yet stand upon the earth, springs, Maurice thought, from the very heart of humanity. Was he mistaken in so interpreting the longings of his fellow men?

No one would quarrel with the exponents of other faiths for starting from their own faiths as a standard. Indeed the comparison of one's own religion with the religions of other folk is a test to which the mature believer in any religion should submit his faith. If he assumes that the elements which other religions possess in common with his own are the vital truths of those other religions, and

that the other elements are excrescences, he stultifies his
enquiry from the start. But this is certainly not a fair
description of Maurice's method. It is true that the
feature of Islam which seems to him most vital is a faith
in the living and eternal God which the Moslem holds in
common with Jew and Christian. But is he mistaken in
thinking that this is the spiritual mainspring of Islam?
And does he assume that this is the most vital merely
because it is a truth common to three religions? And does
he treat other features of Islam as excrescences? I cannot
see how anyone can fairly answer these questions in the
affirmative. Nor does Maurice's treatment of Hinduism
and Buddhism bear out Leslie Stephen's description of his
method, although he tends to exaggerate the affinities
between Christianity and the religions of India. If anything, Maurice is inclined to be too generous in his
estimate of other faiths rather than restricted in his
appreciation by regarding his own faith as the ultimate
standard. Actually, the dangers of misrepresentation in
such an enquiry are rather different from those suggested
by Leslie Stephen. One danger is that we are tempted
to alter the character of our own faith in order to claim
that it does justice in advance to something which we
realise is distinctive and vital in another faith. Another
danger is that we treat only common truths as vital and
treat whatever is distinctive of any of the faiths compared
as of little or no account. Maurice did not succumb to
either of these temptations. If he finds in other religions
dim perceptions of the truth, that Christ is the light of the
world, and He is the Personal Centre of the Universe,
the daysman or umpire between God and man, he may
read too much into them, but I think his work sub-
stantiates his claim that the Christian can be much more

kind and tolerant towards other faiths than any thinker who has no such centre.

What then of the appeal to history? Leslie Stephen thinks that if Maurice's claim for Christianity, based on his analysis, be correct, it should be writ large in current history. If Christianity is not hailed with satisfaction by men of other religious traditions, the claim that Christianity meets all their real needs must be disallowed. Leslie Stephen accuses Maurice of evading the test to which he has appealed and of not understanding what is involved in an appeal to history. Instead of showing that Christianity has given and is giving this satisfaction, Maurice proceeds to say that men ought to find this satisfaction in Christianity or that they would find it if Christianity were properly presented to them. But in my judgment Leslie Stephen himself was mistaken as to the nature of an appeal to history. Maurice cannot be refuted by pointing out the obvious fact that Christianity is not, as yet, the accepted religion of the world. Maurice knew that as well as Leslie Stephen or anyone else. The historical evidence in support of his thesis must necessarily be of another order. It will be found, if it is available, in the history of religions and in the records of conversion, both individual and group conversion.[1] If you find Hindus believing readily and eagerly in Incarnations, and seeking salvation by Bhakti, i.e. by personal devotion to a personal God, if you find that the *Gita* holds a place in Hindu religious life and thought that surpasses the appeal of the Vedanta philosophy, you may begin to suspect that the longing for a Saviour will be found to be the deepest

[1] 'The belief that Jesus has made a real revelation of God rests on the evidence of lives devoted to testing it since Pilate ruled over Judæa, in every continent and by men of the most widely different antecedents, in race, culture, and religion.' T. R. Glover, *Jesus in the Experience of Men*, p. 109.

and most universal exigency of man's nature. If Maurice
had known the difference between Buddhism in Ceylon
and Buddhism in China, between the Hinayana and the
Mahayana, he could have reinforced his argument. Either
the Buddha or the Goddess of Mercy, or the Bodhisattva,
the Buddha to come, is forced to take the central place
which Buddha disclaimed for himself in his original
teaching.[1]

If the history of religions demonstrates this need of a
Saviour, this longing for a Saviour, the records of conversion afford some ground for believing that Jesus satisfies
this need as none other does. Some obiter dicta of a
Japanese professor, reported in a letter many years ago,
will illustrate this contention. 'Jesus speaks very free and
glibly.[2] His logic is about life. After him it became
dogma. Modern logic is about the dead world. He sees

---

[1] W. E. Hocking, in *Living Religions and a World Faith*, p. 193, relates an
incident which is illuminating. He says:
One day I was visiting, with a companion of unimpeachable orthodoxy,
the temple of the Sleeping Buddha near Colombo. A woman was praying,
not at the immense recumbent image of the Buddha, but at a small standing
image at its feet. We questioned the attendant priest. 'Do you not pray to
the Buddha?' 'No; the Buddha has entered Nirvana: he is no longer
concerned with the affairs of this earth.' 'To whom do you pray?' 'To
the Bodhisattvas. This standing image represents a Bodhisattva. He is now
in the Universe, and will some day come to the earth to renew the knowledge
of the truth, which men are always forgetting.' 'Does that coming of the
Bodhisattva mean anything to you?' asked my companion. 'O yes. When
he comes, there will be an end of war and hatred: there will be a time of
peace and kindness. I hope for his coming. I long for his coming!' There
was fervour in the answer. To my surprise, my orthodox companion said,
'I join in your hope!' He had swiftly accepted, across wide differences of
concepts and imagery, an identity of meaning: to this extent he was
coming upon the essence of a symbol common to the two faiths.
  Maurice might have seen in the Buddhist's hope, not the equivalent of
the Christian hope but nevertheless a real confirmation of it.
[2] Cf. the saying of Pascal: 'Jesus utters the deepest truths as if He had
never had to think about them.'

things like the Japanese do.' A hasty conclusion, you say? Yet it holds out the hope that some day the Japanese will see things as He does! Men of all races say the same. Jesus speaks to the condition of every nation. One abiding impression of the World Missionary Conference at Tambaram is that there are now Christ's free men in every land.

Maurice did not attempt to set out the historical evidence as it might be set out to-day. But his belief in the universality of Christ was justified when he wrote. He found here the mainspring of missionary endeavour. I may conclude this chapter with his answer to a plea which is still heard in many quarters, the plea which a business man once put in this form: 'we should make sure of the home market before extending operations abroad'. 'There are heathen at our own doors; we ourselves are half-heathen: leave Buddhists and Mahometans till you have provided for these.' Maurice's answer is two-fold. His first point is, that contacts between East and West are unavoidable. We may not force our commerce on them and take our science to them and at the same time withhold the Gospel. His second, more important consideration lies in the nature of the Gospel itself. 'A faith which boasts to be for humanity cannot test its strength unless it is content to deal with men in all possible conditions. If it limits itself to England, it will adapt itself to the habits and fashions and prejudices of England, of England, too, in a particular age. But doing this, it will never reach the hearts of Englishmen.' The Gospel is addressed to us as men, not as members of a particular nation or a particular class. The Gospel is not ours to keep to ourselves. The missionary enterprise is the sovereign corrective of those prejudices of national- and class-consciousness wherewith otherwise we corrupt the faith.

CHAPTER V

THE THEOLOGICAL ESSAYS

WHEN Maurice published his *Theological Essays* in the
summer of 1853, he expected to get into trouble and his
expectations were not disappointed. In July, he wrote to
Kingsley: 'I knew when I wrote the sentences about
eternal death that I was writing my own sentence at
King's College. And so it will be. Jelf (the Principal) is
behaving very fairly, even kindly: but the issue is quite
certain.' So he was not surprised at the resolution
adopted by the Council of the College on 27 October,
which declared that the references to future punishment in
the essays were of dangerous tendency and calculated to
unsettle the minds of theological students at King's
College. The Council advised the severance of Mr
Maurice's connection with the College, while testifying
to the zealous and able manner in which he had discharged
his duties as professor. It will be noticed that the resolution does not go so far as to denounce Maurice's teaching
as unorthodox or heretical, but merely as dangerous and
unsettling. The majority who adopted the resolution
evidently hoped to avoid a more definite theological
pronouncement, and by the mildness of their censure to
persuade Maurice quietly to withdraw from his professorial chairs (he was Professor of History as well as of
Theology), and save them from the odium of dismissing
him. The resolution reflects the diplomacy of the Bishop
of London (Dr C. J. Blomfield), but Gladstone believed

94

the Bishop would have accepted an amendment which he proposed, if sufficient support for it had been forthcoming. Gladstone moved an amendment requesting the Bishop to appoint a special Committee to examine the *Essays*. He and others thought that the Council was acting with indecent haste and also that the Council was not the right body to pronounce on a theological issue. The actual proceeding of the Council, Gladstone said, was due to a body of laymen, chiefly Lords, among whom that staunch Evangelical, Lord Radstock, was prominent. The persistent attacks on Maurice in *The Record* really precipitated the crisis. Dr Jelf was very sensitive to the attitude of the religious press, and he honestly and naturally thought that the interests and reputation of the College would suffer unless some action were taken. He had for some time been uneasy about Maurice's reputation in orthodox circles. The *Quarterly Review* had subjected Maurice to violent attacks in 1850 and 1851. On the first occasion, the character of the teaching he gave and encouraged others to give to women students at Queen's College had been severely criticised. He had defended himself and his colleagues in a vigorous letter addressed to the Bishop of London. Then in 1851 after Maurice and Kingsley had identified themselves with Christian Socialism, J. W. Croker, who had a personal animus against Maurice, wrote a slashing article in the *Quarterly* denouncing Socialism as the evil of the age and accusing Maurice and Kingsley of fomenting infidelity and anarchy. Dr Jelf had taken alarm then and had urged Maurice to be cautious. The publication of the *Theological Essays* seemed to Dr Jelf clear evidence that Maurice had thrown caution to the winds and was incapable of taking advice. The agitated Principal also saw a connection between Maurice's denial that eternal punishment meant endless torment and his championship of Christian Socialism. Both sentiments savoured of Anabaptism! For the noble Lords on the Council of the College Maurice's Socialist sympathies counted against him. Sir Benjamin Brodie who supported Gladstone's amendment observed, 'It would have been very much better if he (F. D. Maurice) had avoided connecting himself with the Christian Socialists, and discussing questions on which it was plain that persons having great influence in the College would be at variance with him.' Maurice was not prepared to modify his teaching either to conciliate the public opinion represented by the religious press or to avoid hurting the susceptibilities of the governing body of the College. Nor would he make things easy for them by resigning. To resign would be tantamount to admitting that his teaching was not in conformity with the Creeds and the Articles, and also to accepting the view that in subscribing to the Articles he was obliged to accept them in the sense in which they were understood by Dr Jelf and the Council of the College. As far back as 1844 he had protested against the Statute proposed to Convocation in Oxford that the Vice-Chancellor should be authorised to call at any time upon any member of the University to declare that in signing the Articles he took them in the sense in which 'they were both first published and were now imposed by the University'. His tract contributed to the storm of protest which led to the dropping of the proposal. He believed that a man might sign the Articles sincerely if he could give an honest and defensible interpretation of them. No one was obliged to accept them in the sense in which they were first published, or in the sense in which they were now imposed by the University. Neither sense could be easily or assuredly determined, and the agreement between these two senses could not be assumed and was extremely improbable. For himself Maurice pointed out that he understood the reference to 'eternal life' in Article VII in a manner in which the Reformers probably did not intend it. But his view, he maintained, had both Scriptural and Patristic authority behind it. Incidentally, his views on the meaning of the terms 'eternal life' and 'eternal punishment' had been indicated in this pamphlet before he had been appointed to the Chair of Theology at King's College. If they had not been a bar to his appointment, they ought not to be made the ground of his resignation. In the interests alike of truth and of the liberty of the teaching profession, he would not resign. So the Council, adhering to its resolution, took the further step of declaring his Chairs vacant on 11 November 1853.

The doctrine which gave such offence is contained in the concluding essay on Eternal Life and Eternal Death. Maurice starts from the growing repugnance felt among thoughtful people for the doctrine of endless punishment. Those who object to it—and who does not?—point to the appalling fact that anticipations of endless torment in the life to come belong to the New Testament rather than the Old, to the Gospel rather than the Law. Somewhat similarly the Reformation has intensified the horror of the doctrine by removing the relief afforded by belief in the intermediate state of purgatory. And now ardent Evangelicals are inclined to make it an essential article of the faith, a test of orthodoxy, a truth for which the Church must stand or else she will fall. Nevertheless, the laity do not think the clergy really believe the doctrine.

They do not think that we put faith in our own denuncia
tions. They ask, how it is possible for us to go about and
enjoy life if we do; how, if we do, we can look out upon the
world that is around us and the world that has been, without
cursing the day on which we were born? They say that we
pronounce a general sentence, and then explain it away in
each particular case; they say, that we believe that God
condemns the world generally, but that under cover of
certain phrases which may mean anything or nothing, we can
prove that, on the whole, He rather intends it good than ill
... Cultivated men, I say, repeat these things to one another
If we do not commonly hear them, it is because they count it
rude ever to tell us what they think. Poor men say these same
things in their own assemblies with more breadth and honesty
not wishing us to be ignorant of their opinions respecting us.

Maurice, then, by his contacts with men of all classes
but more particularly by his contacts with the workers
was convinced that popular orthodoxy was producing
infidelity and was a growing burden on sensitive spirits
He was concerned to bring relief to this situation.

He begins with a discussion of the words 'eternity' and
'eternal' as used of God. After pointing out that God is
eternal in the sense of being without beginning as well as
without end, he suggests that endless is not an adequate
rendering of eternal or everlasting. 'Eternal', 'ever
lasting', mean something more, something other than
'endless'. Indeed, Eternity in relation to God has
nothing to do with time or duration. Must we not then
say that in reference to life or to punishment, it has
nothing to do with time or duration?

The strength of Maurice's position lay in his recovery
of the true meaning of life eternal in the Johannine
writings. Here I might cite a judicious summary of the
evidence by Mr Brabant:

In St John's Gospel ζωὴ αἰώνιος is, of course, regarded as spiritual—as the Life of the Age, in which all things are spiritual. Its quality is stressed far more than its quantity; its very definition is 'to know the Father and the Son' (xvii. 3); nevertheless, the thought of lastingness is not absent; it is contrasted with the earthly water which perishes (iv. 14); with the wheat which is consumed (iv. 36); with the bread that gives life in this world-order (vi. 54). How far it is eschatological it is hard to say; in some cases the view that eternal life begins 'here and now' is the consequence rather than the content of the Johannine sayings.[1]

J. D. McClure, the former Headmaster of Mill Hill, used to propose reversing the petitions, 'granting us in this world knowledge of thy truth, and in the world to come, life everlasting'. Might we not pray, 'granting us in this world life everlasting and in the world to come knowledge of thy truth'? But indeed if we listen to St John we should refuse to separate knowledge and life in this way. 'This is life eternal to know Thee, the only true God and Jesus Christ whom thou hast sent.' So our prayer should run, 'granting us in this world and in the world to come the knowledge of thy truth which is life eternal'. Certainly, the gift of eternal life cannot be just the assurance of a continued existence after death. The point is strangely misapprehended in J. B. Bury's *History of Freedom of Thought*. He opines that if psychical research brought convincing evidence of communications from the dead, the Gospel as the guarantee of immortality would cease to interest us. But eternal life is not endless duration in time. It is life of a spiritual order, and if on the evidence of psychical research we had more

---

[1] Such texts as Jn. xii. 50 and 1 Jn. iii. 15 suggest it as present. Eternal life and eternal death are to be known here and now.

confidence in an existence beyond the grave, that life
would still need to be redeemed.

It is precisely because the Gospel is concerned with
eternal life in this sense, that the New Testament speaks of
eternal death, of perdition, and eternal punishment.
Summarising Maurice, Leslie Stephen writes: 'God's
punishments are not excessive, for eternity, as we know,
has nothing to do with time, and therefore eternal damna-
tion means *merely* separation from the Eternal.' How
shocked Maurice would have been at this use of the
adverb 'merely' and how clearly it reveals Leslie
Stephen's difficulty in appreciating Maurice! This is how
Maurice himself interpreted what one might term the
severity of the New Testament.

Is it inconsistent, then, with the general object and character
of the New Testament, as the manifestation of His love, that
Eternity in all its aspects should come before us there as it does
nowhere else, that there we should be taught what it means?
Is it inconsistent with its scope and object that there, too, we
should be taught what the horror and awefulness is, of being
without this love, of setting ourselves in opposition to it?
Those who would not own Christ in His brethren, who did
not visit Him when they were sick and in prison, go away,
He said, into eternal or everlasting punishment. Are we
affixing a new meaning to these words, or the very meaning
which the context demands, the only meaning which is consistent with the force that is given to the adjective by our
Lord and His apostles elsewhere, if we say that the eternal
punishment is the punishment of being without the knowledge
of God, who is love, and of Jesus Christ who had manifested
it; even as eternal life is declared to be the having of the
knowledge of God and of Jesus Christ?

Indeed, separation may be worse than active punishment. 'I use both words, *Death* and *Punishment*, that I

may not appear to shrink from the sense which is contained in either. Punishment, I believe, seems to most men less dreadful than death, because they cannot separate it from a punisher, because they believe, however faintly, that He who is punishing them is a Father. The thought of His ceasing to punish them, of His letting them alone, of His leaving them to themselves, is the real, the unutterable horror.' Eternal life and eternal death are set before us as conditions into which we enter here and now, not as rewards and punishments that await us hereafter. 'The state of eternal life and eternal death is not one we can refer only to the future or that we can in any wise identify with the future. Every man who knows what it is to have been in a state of sin, knows what it is to have been in a state of death.' In this Maurice would have agreed with George Fox and his views on election and reprobation. When challenged by a judge who asked whether he believed in election and reprobation, Fox replied, I do, and thou art in the reprobation. When the judge lost his temper, both because Fox addressed him as thou, and declared him reprobate, Fox appealed to his state of mind as evidence of his spiritual condition. But when Fox spoke of reprobation he did not mean lost eternally, but in a state of eternal death from which the light and love of God could still deliver a man.

Maurice, it was assumed, must be committed to Universalism, if he questioned endless punishment. He was indeed thankful that one of the original Forty-two Articles, which expressly condemned universalism, had been scrapped when the Articles were reduced to thirty-nine. But he was thankful because it implied hesitation to pronounce on so difficult an issue. For himself as for Dean Farrar, Eternal Hope seemed the limit of justifiable affirmation. Here is his statement of his position. 'I ask no one to pronounce, for I dare not pronounce myself, what are the possibilities of resistance in a human will to the loving will of God. There are times when they seem to me—thinking of myself more than of others—almost infinite. But I know that there is something which must be infinite. I am obliged to believe in an abyss of love which is deeper than the abyss of death: I dare not lose faith in that love. I sink into death, eternal death if I do. I must feel that this love is compassing the universe. More about it I cannot know. But God knows. I leave myself and all to Him.' This passage seems to echo another great saying of George Fox: 'I saw a great ocean of darkness and death, and again I saw a great ocean of light and life which flowed over the ocean of darkness and death.'

Before passing on to another important feature of the *Essays* which drew forth heated criticism, namely, Maurice's interpretation of the Atonement, we may note two points in his discussion of eternal punishment.

In the first place, Dr Edwyn Bevan, in his Gifford Lectures, challenged the language so commonly used in Christian theology, 'to the effect that the eternity attributed to God is not Time infinitely prolonged, but something wholly different from Time, different not in quantity, but in quality'. 'All this language has come into Christian theology from the Greek Neo-Platonic infiltration. There is nothing in the Jewish or Christian Scriptures to support it.' Then Dr Bevan added, 'The theory, made popular in theological circles by F. D. Maurice, that ζωὴ αἰώνιος means something different from endless time, is not, I believe, confirmed by a study of the use of the term in the Hellenistic Greek spoken and written by contemporary Jews' (p. 97). Dr Bevan's Giffords preceded Mr Brabant's Bamptons, and in the light of Mr Brabant's discussion, Dr Bevan might have modified his judgment. Maurice undoubtedly went too far in declaring that 'eternal' as used in the Scriptures has nothing to do with time or duration. But he was justified in claiming that in St John's writings eternal life does differ from temporal existence in quality rather than in quantity.

In the second place, since his own view of the state of the finally impenitent was to him an unutterable horror, it is rather strange that Maurice did not consider more sympathetically the theory of conditional immorality, which in his lifetime was advocated by Edward White and which later secured the powerful adhesion of Dr Dale.[1] Maurice had, however, closed the avenue that might have led him to it. In commenting on the passage, 'Be not afraid of them which kill the body and after that have no more that they can do: but I will forewarn you whom ye shall fear: Fear him which, after he hath killed, hath power to cast into hell, yea, I say unto you, fear him', Maurice anticipated the interpretation which commended itself to Miss Lily Dougall and Dr Emmet in *The Lord of Thought*. The one who has power to cast into hell and whom we are to fear, is the Devil not God. Maurice asks whether the accepted interpretation 'which has become so familiar that one hears it without even a hint that there is another, does not show us on the edge of what an abyss we are standing, how likely we are to confound the Father of lights with the Spirit of darkness?' But the evidence of Rabbinic parallels[2] is against

---

[1] See Dale's *Life*, pp. 311–13.

[2] In *Studies in Pharisaism and the Gospels*, 2nd series, Israel Abrahams points out that the phraseology in Matthew x. 28 and Luke xii. 4 is Hebraic, and he cites at length from the Talmud the interesting story of Rabban

Maurice's interpretation, and even if the one who has authority to cast into hell is the Devil, the authority is derived from God. Matthew's version, 'fear him who is able to destroy both body and soul in Gehenna' is clearly in line with Rabbinic teaching, as Professor Manson points out, and the closest parallel asserts conditional immortality. 'The wicked of Israel in their bodies and the wicked of the nations of the world in their bodies go down to hell, and are punished in it for twelve months. After twelve months, their souls become extinct and their bodies are burned up and hell casts them out and they turn to ashes and the wind scatters them and strews them beneath the soles of the feet of the righteous.'[1] It is curious to find Ibsen's whimsical idea of the button-maker in *Peer Gynt* has support in that this saying of Jesus is best understood as an assertion of the absolute sovereignty of God and as implying conditional immortality. But if Maurice had known the parallels and realised the implication he might still have clung to the larger hope. I think he would have approved that striking saying of Charles Péguy, 'What will God say to us, if some of us go to Him without the others?'

It is also appropriate to add a word on the paradox of Maurice's defence of the Athanasian creed, which so

Johanan ben Zakkai, whose disciples found him in tears when they visited him during an illness. When they asked him the reason for his weeping, he replied that if he were being led into the presence of a human being, a judge or a king, even then he might weep, 'but now when I am being led into the presence of the King of Kings, the Holy One, blessed be He, ... Who if He be wrathful against me, His wrath is eternal...Who if He condemned me to death, the death would be for ever, ...nay more when before me lie two ways, one to the garden of Eden, and the other of Gehinnom, and I know not in which I am to be led—shall I not weep?' (op. cit., p. 47). It seems clear from this parallel that 'He who has power to destroy both body and soul' is to be identified with God.

[1] *The Mission and Message of Jesus*, p. 399.

shocked Leslie Stephen. Leslie Stephen wrote: 'Not long before his death Mr Maurice published a remarkable defence of the Athanasian Creed. That document commended itself to him as an unequivocal protest against dogmatism and uncharitableness. The ordinary reader was simply bewildered by such utterances. If the Athanasian tenets be not dogmas and damning those who disbelieve them, not uncharitable, dogma and charity are words without sense.' But however paradoxical, the line of Maurice's defence is clear enough. If to know the only true God and Jesus Christ whom He has sent be eternal life, then men cannot enter into life without that knowledge. If the Athanasian Creed, so-called, sets forth the essential nature of God and of God's love, then this is part of the knowledge in which stands our eternal life. Then to warn men that without it they will be lost is simple charity. The steps in this argument may or may not convince us, but they are intelligible, and in justice to Maurice it should be added that he was well aware that if the damnatory clauses expressed a dogmatic overbearing temper in the author or authors of the creed, they could not be defended.

If Maurice's views on Eternal Punishment lost him his Chairs at King's College, his views on the Atonement got him into trouble over the border. Westcott was surprised that Maurice's views on the Atonement did not arouse more discussion in England. But Scottish theologians were quickly on his track, scenting in him the heresies of Thomas Erskine and McLeod Campbell. Dr Candlish addressed a crowded meeting of the Y.M.C.A. in London in February 1854, and demonstrated to his own satisfaction and to that of his audience the theological incompetence of Maurice. The head and front of Maurice's offence was that, following St Paul, he regarded God as the author and not as the object of propitiation. He denied that Christ bore the punishment of sin or that He died to satisfy the just demands of the Law. He insisted that Christ died to save us from sin, not from the punishment of sin. All orthodox schools have believed that He rescued men out of the power of an enemy by yielding to his power, not that He rescued them out of the hand of God by paying a penalty to Him. We read in the Fourth Gospel Christ said, 'Therefore doth my Father love me because I lay down my life for the sheep.' 'How then can we tolerate for an instant that notion of God which would represent Him as satisfied by the punishment of sin, not by the purity and graciousness of the Son?' Actually, the chapter on the Atonement is neither very full nor very clear. Maurice handled the theme more effectively in his sermons on the doctrine of Sacrifice. There he makes the following comment on the idea of propitiation. 'But the theory of a propitiation, not set forth by God, but devised to influence His mind—of a propitiation that does not declare God's righteousness *in* the forgiveness of sins, but which makes it possible for Him to forgive sins, *though* He is righteous—this scheme changes all the relations of the Creator and creature; this scheme does build up a priestcraft which subverts utterly the morality of the Bible, because it first subverts its theology.'

All this was anathema to Dr Candlish. Nothing but the old substitutionary view of the Atonement seemed to him tenable. The Atonement is the satisfaction of the justice of the divine judge. The thought of God as judge is the essential truth. 'I stand for the authority of God as Judge in the plain English meaning of the word, judge. I stand for the authority of His law and its sanctions: apart from which I see no hope for earth, no security against heaven itself becoming as hell. A theology without law—law in the condemnation—law in the atonement—law in the justification—law in the judgment—is to me like the universal return of chaos and old night.' Christ died to relieve the distress of guilty sinners, oppressed by the sense of the righteous arm of a Lawgiver and Judge holding them fast. 'When God justifies, He summons the offender before Him, and looking upon him as one by faith with His own righteous Son acquits and accepts him accordingly.'

A less conventional Calvinist, old Rabbi Duncan of the *Colloquia Peripatetica*, thought Maurice neglected Law and substituted ethicism for Law. 'Maurice's system [he once said] is pure illegality. It will never go down with the lawyers. Paul started from the principle, The law is good. He never set himself up as the equal of his maker. But this is the upshot of the sentimental system lately revived in England.'

Possibly to-day we may be more sympathetic in our judgment on forensic theology than were Maurice and other Victorians. We realise that old Dr Candlish had good reason for suggesting that the breakdown of Law would mean the return of chaos and black night. When William of Orange entered London after the flight of King James, he was welcomed on behalf of the legal profession by the oldest member of the Bench, a judge aged ninety-one. When William congratulated him on having outlived his contemporaries, the old man replied, 'And if your Highness had not come over, I should have outlived the Law itself!' The breakdown of Law is an unmitigated disaster. Hitler used the war as an excuse to remove the last vestige of judicial restraint on arbitrary power in Germany. There is a growing rapprochement in Germany between the Churches and the Social Democratic workers, because they have discovered a common interest in securing legal protection for the rights of individual citizens and voluntary associations. When thousands have laid down their lives to re-establish the reign of Law, it may not seem outrageous to suggest some connection between Christ's death and the maintenance of Law.

I am also inclined to think that the old substitutionary view of the Atonement may still have a place in pastoral theology. Whether morbid or not, there are states of conscience when we cannot believe in forgiveness unless reparation has been made, and when we know full well that we can never make such reparation ourselves. Though we are offended by the rationalised doctrine, we can still on occasion sing 'Rock of Ages', and mean it.

Yet the recoil from forensic theology was absolutely necessary. The few pages in *Christ in Modern Theology* which Dr Fairbairn devoted to Dr Candlish say all that is necessary, but it needed to be said. To start from the thought of God as Judge, as if it were the fundamental truth about God, is fatal to a true understanding of Him with whom we have to do. The sovereignty of God must not be construed in terms of oriental despotism or even of constitutional monarchy. 'The natural sovereignty is of different order; its representative, or type, is the parent or the patriarch.... The more perfect a father, the more of a sovereign will he be: the better he is as a sovereign, the more excellently will he fulfil his functions as a father. ...The two ideas of paternity and sovereignty are not only compatible, they are inseparable.... While the relations of a sovereign are all legal, the relations of a father are all personal. The punishments of a sovereign aim at the maintenance of order; the punishments of a father are for the good of the offender.'[1] Maurice would have said Amen to all this. He traced the beginnings of law and sovereignty to the position of the father in the family, not so much to the *patria potestas* as the *patria auctoritas*. He believed that the punishments of God were remedial or redemptive. Men need and men desire to be freed from sin, not from the punishment of sin. To subordinate the Fatherhood of God to the sovereignty of God is to make God's relation to us legal and not personal. This is precisely the reversal of the Gospel.

It is arguable that though as Rabbi Duncan reminds us, St Paul declared the law to be good, the apostle nevertheless underrated Law and narrowed its functions too strictly when he regarded it as an interim-expedient to awaken and deepen the sense of sin. In moral education Law has a more positive contribution to make than that. Yet the forensic theology completely misunderstood St Paul. He did not believe that Jesus died to appease an angry God. He did not believe, I think, that Christ bore the punishment of sin. He did not believe that Christ's death satisfied the just claims of the Law so that our past sins once forgiven, we might have another chance to try to live up to the Law. Just as Maurice recovered the Johannine conception of eternal life, so he went a long way towards recovering the true Pauline conception of the Atonement.

When St Paul told the Romans, that Christ is the end of law to everyone that believes, he meant what he said. Christ died to set men free from the dominance of legal concepts in their relation to God. He died to end the

---

[1] *Christ in Modern Theology*, pp. 432–6.

dream of the self-made man, the dream of a self-achieved, self-satisfied righteousness, to teach us that 'merit lives from man to man and not from man, O Lord, to Thee'. He died that men should no longer live as the slaves of a task-master God but as children in their Father's house. He died, because only at this cost could some be convinced of the possibility of living as God's children, and because others assumed the privilege too readily and esteemed it too lightly. Then I am sure Maurice was interpreting St Paul aright in insisting on salvation from sin rather than from the punishment of sin. The wrath of God in Romans i, is a process of social demoralisation which destroys intellectual as well as moral integrity. The righteousness of God must reverse the process. I remember hearing Lord Lindsay of Birker say of the death of Socrates that it stopped the moral rot in Greece. In a deeper sense, St Paul claimed that the death of Christ was God's way of stopping the moral rot in the Greco-Roman world. So Christ did not die to appease the wrath of God, the wrath being conceived as some form of extraneous penalty imposed on a sinful world. He died that a world under the wrath of God as clearly seen in its deepening moral failure might become the righteousness of God in Him. St Paul is preoccupied with the thought of the Gospel as the power of God unto salvation. The forensic theology of the Atonement never did justice to what was deepest in his teaching.

Another aspect of the Cross, which meant much to St Paul and is neglected by us, appealed to Maurice. In the Cross, Christ vanquished principalities and powers, stripped them of their dominion over the minds and lives of men. Maurice, like present day Lutheran theologians, reaffirmed belief in a personal Satan. He thought we judged men too harshly, by refusing to recognise the power of the adversary. Likewise, we underrate the salvation Christ has brought, because we discount the victory of the Cross over the powers of evil. There is no question here of a purchase-price paid to the Devil or of a trick played on the Devil. The conviction entertained by St Paul, is that Christ met and overcame all the powers of ill that may assail us in death.

I confess that I do not know whether this belief in a personal Satan is to be retained in all its literalness or treated as a symbol. If it should be treated as a symbol, I am not sure of its interpretation. But since it appealed to Maurice as it certainly did to St Paul, I am not disposed just to set it on one side.

I ought not to suggest that this aspect of St Paul's teaching bulked large in Maurice's mind. He found a wealth of meaning in Christ's sacrifice, which he expounded in his book, *The Doctrine of Sacrifice*, the preface to which contains his reply to Dr Candlish. But without pursuing these controversies further, I would emphasise the starting-point which determined the attitude of Maurice on both the issues discussed in this chapter.

The first of the *Theological Essays* is on Charity. He starts, that is to say, from the love of God. To proclaim the unchanging love of God to men is the first and last duty of the Church. He noted with satisfaction that the Fall of Man does not appear before Article IX in the Articles. The Gospel of the grace of God is not just a remedy for the Fall. God's love is set on men as men, and not just on men as sinners. By the grace of God, Christ tasted death for every man. If we start from the Fall, death is the wages and outcome of sin. But if we recognise the place of death in the economy of nature, it is not simply the outcome of sin. So in tasting death for every man, Christ bears indeed the burden of our sin, but He also bears and shares the burden of our mortality. It is not easy to make clear what seems to be involved in Maurice's insistence that we start from the love of God, but it may be suggested by a phrase in the Nicene Creed. When we speak of the Son of God who for us men and for our salvation became man, the grammarian might say that 'for us men and for our salvation', is a hendiadys or a tautology. But it may suggest that those scholastics were right who believed that the Incarnation would have taken place, had there been no Fall of Man. The Son of God became Son of Man, for us men as well as for our salvation. God loves His children, while they are sinners and while they are enemies. But God loves His children as His children.

One final sentence on this main theme from Maurice himself. Writing to Ludlow about the significance of his stand at King's College he said, 'I must bear what testimony I can for the right of English divines to preach the Gospel of God's love to mankind and to maintain that Lord Shaftesbury and the Bishop of London do not care more for the outcasts of the race than He does. If Humanity and Theology are not to be for ever apart, the regeneration of the working-classes is not to be given up by Christians to infidels. This point must be settled somehow.'

CHAPTER VI

WHAT IS REVELATION?

IN 1858 Mansel, at that time reader in moral and meta-physical philosophy at Magdalen College, and later Dean of St Paul's, delivered the Bampton lectures, taking as his subject 'The Limits of Religious Thought'. In spite of and perhaps because of their abstract and metaphysical character, the lectures were immensely popular at the time of their delivery. The popularity did not last and they have since been unduly neglected.[1] It is pleasant to find Edwyn Bevan devoting one of his Gifford lectures to a sympathetic critique of Mansel's position. But to Maurice, Mansel's attempt to defend a conventional orthodoxy with the weapons of philosophic scepticism seemed anathema, and as soon as the lectures appeared

---

[1] It is worth while to recall the fact that Mansel's book made a strong appeal to Alexander Whyte, who was a student at King's College, Aberdeen, at the time of the Mansel-Maurice controversy. Whyte bought the *Bampton Lectures* in the spring of 1860. He thought it 'a noble book, but a stiff one'. His sympathies were with Mansel in the controversy, perhaps because Mansel's position safeguards the sovereignty of God. But as his biographer says, Whyte 'was carried along by the author's wide knowledge, clear style, and well-ordered argument. He believed that he had here found a way of reconciling the older theology with the intellectual conception of the infinity of the Divine Nature. To the dangers of Mansel's sharp division of Faith from speculative Knowledge he does not seem to have been fully awake.' While he thus came down on Mansel's side, Alexander Whyte rejoiced to believe that the controversialists were at one in their 'return to the cardinal doctrine of a personal living Christ'. Dr G. F. Barbour's account of Alexander Whyte's reaction to the controversy in his *Life of Alexander Whyte*, pp. 70–5, should not be overlooked by anyone interested in the history of religious thought in the Victorian Era.

in print he subjected them to a detailed criticism in a series of letters to a theological student, which were published in 1859 in a volume entitled, *What is Revelation?*

The tone and temper of his criticism left something to be desired. Leslie Stephen says that as Mansel's apologetic struck at the primary assumptions of Mr Maurice's method, 'it is not wonderful that, for once in his life, he was betrayed into an angry controversy'. 'The anger indeed was returned with interest: and Dean Mansel went so far as to charge his antagonist with wilful lying.' Leslie Stephen adds: 'Cooler observers would only remark that misunderstandings were inevitable on both sides when issue was joined between two reasoners who had not one principle in common.'

Maurice indeed started with a prejudice against Mansel. Archbishop Thomson, who had heard one of the lectures, described the course as 'in its essence the most unalloyed Atheism that had been heard in England for generations'. That judgment was sufficiently disturbing. Then the popularity of the lectures turned in part on the clarity and wit with which Mansel expounded his philosophical position. An audience is always flattered when a philosopher is so lucid that his hearers think they understand, and so witty that they know they are entertained. Mansel was a devastating critic. Philosophers and theologians of any and every school went down like ninepins, and Martineau describes 'the appendix of notes to the lectures as a miscellaneous prison-house where all evil spirits are reserved for judgement'. At one point in *What is Revelation?* Maurice makes a catalogue of these evil spirits who are condemned for Dogmatism or Rationalism or both. It includes among the more notable, Schleiermacher, Hegel, Strauss, Anselm, Jowett, Greg, Socinus, Froude,

Priestley, Maurice, Kant, Coleridge, Dorner, Occam, Fichte, Parker, Emerson, Plotinus, Angelus Silesius, Feuerbach, Comte. Callow undergraduates lapped up the lectures, because they served as an excuse for laughing at all troublesome German or English thinkers. Maurice could not believe that Mansel was serious and assumed that he was a Senior Common Room wit playing to the gallery of public opinion. This was unfair to Mansel. A heated criticism based on such an assumption naturally called forth a heated reply and gave offence to Mansel's friends. Maurice's son and biographer says guardedly, 'I do not think any of my father's friends have ever read the discussion with entire satisfaction.' Maurice himself moderated his tone in his *Sequel to What is Revelation?* and in 1871, soon after Mansel's death, he added this note to a new edition of his *Moral and Metaphysical Philosophy*: 'As I had the misfortune many years ago in a book long forgotten to enter into controversy with Dean Mansel, I am anxious to express my regret for any language which I may have used in the course of it which though no wise injurious to his reputation, may have given pain to some of his friends. His immeasurable superiority to me as a disputant deepens my conviction that the principle which I maintained against him was sound and true, one which even his ability and learning could not shake.' Whatever errors in temper and judgment marred Maurice's contribution to this discussion, he was right in regarding it as the most important controversy of his life.[1]

[1] A. V. G. Allen, in *The Continuity of Christian Thought* (p. 422), says: 'The controversy which took place between [Mansel] and Mr Maurice, in which the latter called attention to the question, "What is Revelation?" is perhaps the most significant one in the whole history of the Church since Athanasius stood up to resist the Arians on a similar, if not the same, identical issue.'

The question, What is Revelation? is still a pertinent question and the issues involved are still live issues.

What then were Mansel's main contentions, and why did Maurice react to them so violently?

Assuming, as we must, the existence of God as the First Cause of the Universe and as the Absolute and Infinite Being, Mansel claimed that God's essential nature must remain unknown and unknowable. 'The knowledge of the Absolute and Infinite is made impossible by the very constitution of our minds.' If we cannot form any clear conception of the Absolute and the Infinite or make logically coherent statements regarding the one or the other, it will follow that the confident assertions of the Dogmatists and the rash denials of the Rationalists are alike out of court. In its early days Woodbrooke numbered among its students a very able Dutchman who was by way of being an Hegelian mystic. The discussion circle which he attended was absolutely fogged, because, as the Warden happily observed, 'The dear man was always ballooning about with the Absolute!' Mansel's presence at Woodbrooke at that period would have been most welcome. He was an adept at deflating balloons. It was part of his mission in life to demonstrate that folk who balloon about with the Absolute are liable to talk nonsense.

A metaphysical theology, giving us speculative knowledge of God, being ruled out as unattainable, is there any other way in which we can come to the knowledge of God? Will not the sense of dependence or the sense of duty bring us to our goal? Will not Schleiermacher or Kant or both point the way for us? That the Feeling of Dependence and the Conviction of Moral Obligation have a profound religious significance, Mansel is well aware. They give rise respectively to Prayer and to the sense of sin which seeks relief in Expiation. They form our impressions of the Power and Goodness of God, and compel us to think of God as in some sense personal. But, Mansel contends, we are mistaken in supposing that in the Feeling of Dependence and the Conviction of Moral Obligation we are conscious of the Absolute and Infinite. 'We cannot be conscious of the Infinite: but we can be and are conscious of the limits of our own powers of thought: and therefore we know that the possibility or impossibility of conception is no test of the possibility or impossibility of existence...In this impotence of Reason, we are compelled to take refuge in Faith and to believe that an Infinite Being exists, though we know not how: and that He is the same with that Being who is made known in consciousness as our Sustainer and our Law-giver.' This latter form of knowledge is regulative and not speculative. 'We must be content with those regulative ideas of the Deity, which are sufficient to guide our practice, but not to satisfy our intellect—which tell us, not what God is in Himself, but how He wills that we should think of Him.'

How does God will that we should think of Him? This we can only learn from the Revelation contained in the Scriptures. And this Revelation is not to be judged on its contents but received on the strength of the external evidences, particularly the evidence of miracle. 'The legitimate object of a rational criticism of revealed religion is not to be found in the *contents* of that religion, but in its *evidences*.' 'The only question which we are reasonably at liberty to ask relates to the evidences of the Revelation as a fact. If there is sufficient evidence, on other grounds, to show that the Scripture in which this doctrine is contained, is a Revelation from God, the doctrine itself must be unconditionally received, not as reasonable or unreasonable, but as scriptural.' It is gratifying to a Cambridge man to find an Oxford philosopher advocating a return to Paley and Paley's Evidences. But it is more important to notice that from this standpoint Mansel could defend any doctrine which was generally regarded as part of the Revelation contained in the Scripture. Evangelicals assumed that all their treasured beliefs were now immune from serious criticism. No objections whether advanced by rationalists or mystics or moralists could retain any validity, if Mansel's line of argument held good.

The strength and value of Mansel's position lie, as Edwyn Bevan perceives, in its being a forcible reminder of the symbolic character of our thoughts concerning God. 'Notwithstanding all our confidence of high attainments, all our notions of God are but childish in respect of His infinite perfection. We lisp and babble and say we know not what for the most part, in our most accurate, as we think, conceptions and notions of God.' So declared the Puritan divine, John Owen, at one time Vice-Chancellor of the University of Oxford. He also reminds us that our knowledge of God at the best is like Moses's vision of God's backward parts. 'We know so little of God because it is God who is thus to be known.' Isaac Penington has a similar insight when he says 'All truths are a shadow except the last, though each is true in its own place.' There are close parallels to Mansel's position in some forms of modern dialectical theology. There are also close and disconcerting parallels in the logical positivism of Professor A. J. Ayer. Nevertheless, the insistence on a reverent agnosticism as a constituent element in religious faith is justified and is of service to-day.

Mansel's use of this in itself wholesome agnosticism for apologetic purposes is however much more questionable. Leslie Stephen observes: 'Most critics have considered this to be a dangerous line of argument, and even hold that it leads more logically to Atheism or to Positivism than to Christianity.' Actually it leads logically to the agnosticism of Herbert Spencer, as Maurice anticipated 'when he declared what its inevitable tendency must be, how the weapon forged in behalf of orthodoxy will become a deadly one in other hands'. If God be the Unknowable, as Mansel argues, we must take our stand with Herbert Spencer. As Martineau saw, Mansel's argument proves too much. It proves not that we must accept a revelation but that no revelation is possible. 'That negation should send a message to nescience appears not readily conceivable: nor can we imagine in what the "evidences" for such a communication could consist. Our author's logic then in mowing down its thistle-field inconsiderately mows off its own legs.' The weakness which Martineau detected is connected with Mansel's handling of the idea of the Absolute. The Absolute literally means untied, freed from all ties, and Mansel correctly conceives the Absolute as standing in no *necessary* relation with any finite thing or person. It thus became the assertion of the transcendence of God. But Mansel then interprets the Absolute as standing in no necessary relation with anything, to mean that the Absolute cannot come into relation with anything without ceasing to be the Absolute. If we accept this perverse interpretation, Martineau is right. It proves, not that we must accept a revelation, but that no revelation is possible. If we identify God with the Absolute of Mansel's argument, Herbert Spencer's Unknowable is the last word about God.

The heart of the controversy between Maurice and
Mansel turns on the question, Does God reveal Himself
and in that revelation give us true knowledge of Himself?
But before I concentrate attention on this fundamental
issue, I may recall some other features of Mansel's method
which were distasteful to Maurice. He disliked Mansel's
way of taking the representatives of two extremes and
knocking their heads together. Mansel plays off Dogmatists against Rationalists, and non-suits both of them.
Maurice held that it was more important to discover the
points in which each was right than to make fun of their
manifest errors. He urged that in historical enquiries,
in the case of the conflict between the King and the
Commons in the seventeenth century, for example, 'it is
not by ranging ourselves on either side, least of all is
it by despising both sides and setting up ourselves as
superior to both, that we arrive at the right historical
lesson'. So in theology, particularly in controversial
theology, we need to understand the strong convictions
at the heart of each party to the controversy and do
justice to them. Maurice's comment on Mansel's handling
of Schleiermacher and Hegel is typical of the dissatisfaction which Mansel's method aroused in his mind.

An ordinary English reader of Mr Mansel's book might easily
suppose that Schleiermacher and Hegel exhibit the same habit
of mind in different measures. He could scarcely conjecture
that they were direct opponents: that Hegelism is fled to by
numbers just because the Consciousness of Schleiermacher is
felt to be unsatisfactory, because it is thought to make Truth
dependent upon our feelings instead of being fixed and eternal:
that Schleiermacher is fled to by numbers because Hegel's
absolute teaching appears to be hard and inhuman. A fair
examination of *this* conflict might surely avail to make us feel

what is weak and wanting in each, and to prevent us from accepting the dogmas of either, than a denunciation of both.[1]

Such a fair examination of conflicting views Maurice was always seeking. The apparent absence from Mansel's book of any such appreciation of opposites he continually deplores.

Another feature of Mansel's method which aroused distrust was his reliance on the type of apologetic which is best exemplified in Butler's *Analogy*. I have never regretted that in my teens my father persuaded me with a bribe of half-a-crown to read Butler's *Analogy*, in a rather forbidding edition with notes, prepared by Dr Angus for students at Regent's Park College. But the argument of the *Analogy* has a very limited scope. The Butler of the *Sermons* is more worth while than the Butler of the *Analogy*. For in the *Analogy*, the argument is little more than this, that the difficulties which the Deists find in the revealed religion which they reject are to be found in equal seriousness in the natural religion which they accept. Butler aims to convince the Deist that if he accepts natural religion he should also accept revealed religion. The argument might lead to an opposite conclusion, that if he rejects revealed religion, he ought also to reject natural religion. There is, however, some service in pointing out that the difficulties men find in revealed religion are present also in the natural order. Mansel's suggestion that the mystery of the two natures, divine and human, in Christ is as difficult to understand and as easy to accept as the mystery of mind and body and their interaction, is not without its value. But to Maurice, as to

---

[1] *What is Revelation?*, pp. 295–6.

Martineau, the *Analogy* seems a poor way of commending a revelation. Men will hardly be persuaded to accept a revelation because its mysteries and difficulties are no greater and no less than those we find in natural religion and in the constitution and course of nature. Surely, a revelation is intended to clear up difficulties and throw light on mysteries. If it does not do that, is it really revelation?

Much more serious objections emerge when we turn to Mansel's conception of the revelation contained in the Scriptures. Mansel clearly conceives revelation as consisting primarily of doctrines, statements of truths which we are to believe. In the Scriptures, God literally tells us what to think. Mansel might not have accepted so crude a statement, though this is the only possible meaning of revelation according to Dr Candlish. Revelation is the Word of God, in the sense of verbal communications from the Almighty. If Mansel did not so understand Revelation, he gave no hint of an alternative view. Revelation then consists of doctrines, and the doctrines which constitute the scriptural revelation coincide with the tenets of traditional orthodoxy. Thus in the first lecture Mansel refers to 'the revealed doctrine of Christ's Atonement for the sins of man' and leaves the reader to infer that the revealed doctrine is the current substitutionary view of the Atonement. This is part of the Revelation which must be unconditionally received, not as reasonable or unreasonable but as scriptural. On this Maurice notes that the lecturer does not waste a single line in telling us what the revealed doctrine of Christ's Atonement is. 'Mr Mansel must have had a very strong suspicion that if he *had* stated the revealed doctrine of the Atonement according to his notion of it, a number of the most earnest, the most confessedly orthodox and Evangelical clergymen in England would have said either "We do not accept it in that sense" or "That method of setting it forth does not satisfy us", or "Such an explanation may do very well for the schools, but it is not the doctrine to preach in our pulpits to sinners."' Mansel certainly allowed his hearers and readers to assume that his views of the doctrines revealed in Scripture coincided with theirs. But if the essence of the Scripture revelation is to be found in doctrinal statements, we cannot equate it with traditional orthodoxy. We cannot assume that it is properly represented in the Biblical theology of Calvin's *Institutes* or the systematic theology of Dr Hodge. And incidentally, we cannot accept doctrines unconditionally as scriptural, whether they be reasonable or not. The old woman who believed that the whale swallowed Jonah because the Scriptures say so, and who would have believed Jonah swallowed the whale if the Scriptures had said so, was not exhibiting her faith. There are indeed times when God leads the blind by a way they know not, but a revelation that did not appeal to our reason would not be a revelation at all. In any case, if the Scripture contains revealed doctrines, reason must try to understand and justify them. But is Revelation primarily the communication to men of a body of doctrines?

As I suggested in an earlier chapter, the difficulty of understanding Maurice, the difficulty felt by orthodox theologians like Dr Candlish and agnostics like Leslie Stephen, was that he no longer regarded revelation as truth communicated in propositions. Leslie Stephen was right when he said that in dealing with Maurice, 'to bring things to an issue we have to learn not a new set of facts or opinions, but a new mode of thinking'. At least we have to consider a new answer to the question, 'What is Revelation?' Here what Maurice is contending for has since become almost a commonplace. The Bible is a revelation of God in action, it is the record of God's personal dealings with men and nations. It is true that the vision granted to Moses was the vision of God's backward parts, but it is also true that God spake with Moses face to face, as a man speaks with his friend. When Mansel stresses the limits of religious thought, he distinguishes, as we have seen, between speculative truths and regulative truths. The first are truths in the full sense of the word. They constitute exact reasoned knowledge of the reality with which they are concerned. The second are inexact and symbolic. They give us not truth or knowledge in the full sense, but such approximations to truth as may serve as a guide to conduct. In the things of God, man is incapable of arriving at or receiving speculative truths. Revelation and faith must be concerned with regulative truths, with such ideas of God and His relation to us as God wishes us to entertain. Maurice, not altogether fairly, identified this distinction with 'the notion of a revelation that tells us things which are not in themselves true, but which it is right for us to believe and act upon as if they were true'. Mansel repudiated the suggestion that regulative truths are not in themselves true, though they are necessarily imperfect and relative to the mind of the receiver. But he asserted roundly that they were concerned with man's duty and destiny. They constitute 'primarily and properly a knowledge not of God's nature, but of man's obligations'. 'Man does not know God as God knows Himself: hence he does not know Him in the fulness of His Absolute Nature.' Revelation is subject to the limitations which encompass all human thought.

For Maurice, the truth concerning God which comes to us through revelation is neither speculative nor regulative, but personal. Regulative truths would not be regulative, if they were not knowledge of God's nature as well as of man's obligations. Indeed, we cannot know what man's obligations are unless we know what God is. Speculative knowledge of God in Mansel's sense of the term is doubtless out of man's reach, but it is not the kind of knowledge which we seek and desire and need. We have not to choose between knowing God in the fulness of His Absolute Nature and not knowing Him at all or knowing Him in a purely symbolic way. We are to know Him as our Creator and our Redeemer. The doctrine of creation is not a regulative truth, a way in which it is right for us to think of God, though Creator He is not. On the contrary, creation is a fact not a doctrine, and God reveals Himself in the very act of creating. The sense of dependence and the sense of moral obligation alike reveal the real presence of God in human experience. God permits and enables us to know Him as we know our friends. Such knowledge is never speculative and never merely regulative. It is personal and it may be and should be progressive. For just as knowledge of our friends grows through their attitude and conduct under varying circumstances, so we learn the nature of God through events, through His acts, through His saving acts.

R. H. Hutton, reviewing the controversy and writing as a disciple and admirer of Maurice, puts succinctly Maurice's main contentions in one of his *Theological Essays*. He entirely denies Dr Mansel's assumption that direct converse with God implies faculties for constructing a 'theory of God'.[1] This he holds is Mansel's funda-

---

[1] *Theological Essays*, p. 88.

mental error. We may have direct converse with God, a true knowledge of God, without being able to construct an adequate rational speculative theology. Hutton sees likewise that we do not identify God with the Absolute and the Infinite as Mansel conceives them. Mansel holds that the Absolute and the Infinite exclude all limitations or order of all sorts. 'The one alternative which Dr Mansel did not deign to admit into his religious dilemma even hypothetically—that of undiluted energy, conditioned by definite laws, moral and spiritual—is that which the revelation of conscience and the revelation of history alike offer to us as the actual standard of perfection.' But the defect in Mansel's position which seemed to Maurice and Hutton most serious was his assumption that moral standards are merely regulative and relative, and that what is asserted of God in the Scriptures is not to be subjected to the moral standards enjoined upon us. Mansel seems bent on denying the validity of moral as well as of rational criticism in relation to the scriptural revelation. Here Mansel laid himself open to Mill's magnificent protest against admitting as just in the action or character of God anything we should condemn as unjust in the conduct of our fellow men. Maurice joined issue with Mansel on the subject of the duty of forgiveness. 'Man's duty to forgive is grounded not in his likeness but in his unlikeness to God.' So Mansel argued. 'This duty is binding upon man on account of the weakness and ignorance and sinfulness of his nature: that he is bound to forgive as one who himself needs forgiveness: as one whose weakness renders him liable to suffering: as one whose self-love is ever ready to arouse his passions and pervert his judgment.' Both Maurice and Hutton somewhat impatiently criticise what is after all a real ground for impressing the duty of forgiveness upon men. But Mansel seemed to them to ignore or belittle the moral incentive of the Gospel. The good news of the divine forgiveness is the great incentive to human forgiveness. We are to forgive as God in Christ has forgiven us. We are to forgive not because we are like but because thus we may become like our Father in Heaven. In the teaching on forgiveness in the Gospel it is precisely the discovery of God's nature which determines and regulates man's obligation.

The heart of the controversy turns on the character of the revelation of God in Christ. Here the two controversialists were more nearly at one than either realised. Both accepted what has been called the scandal of particularity. 'Men object', so Leslie Stephen assures us, 'to a theory which gives to certain historical facts or to certain special observances a character entirely disparate from that which belongs to all other history and to all natural operations.' Lessing declared that the essence of religion must consist in the eternal truths of reason and cannot depend on the contingent facts of history. So Strauss, as a follower of Hegel, finds in the largely mythical story of Jesus, not a historic incarnation but the symbol of the universal truth that in Humanity, God becomes Man, the infinite manifesting itself in the finite and the finite spirit remembering its infinitude. Against all such metaphysical generalisations, Mansel insisted on the value of historic fact. In what Maurice praised as a passage of great rhetorical power, Mansel wrote:

It is for this idea, so superior to all history and fact—this necessary process of the unconscious and impersonal Infinite— that we are to sacrifice that blessed miracle of Divine Love and Mercy, by which the Son of God, of His own free act and will, took man's nature upon Him for man's redemption. It is for this that we are to obliterate from our faith that touching picture of the pure and holy Jesus, to which mankind for eighteen centuries has ever turned, with the devotion of man to God rendered only more heartfelt by the sympathy of love between man and man: which from generation to generation has nurtured the first seeds of religion in the opening mind of childhood, by the image of that Divine Child who was cradled in the manger of Bethlehem and was subject to His parents at Nazareth: which has checked the fiery temptations of youth by the thought of Him who 'was in all points tempted like as we are, yet without sin': which has consoled man struggling with poverty and sorrow, by the pathetic remembrance of Him who on earth had not where to lay His head: which has blended into one brotherhood the rich and the poor, the mighty and the mean among mankind, by the example of Him who, though He was rich, yet for our sakes became poor: though He was equal with God, yet took upon Him the form of a servant: which has given to the highest and purest precepts of morality an additional weight and sanction, by the records of that life in which the marvellous and the familiar are so strangely yet so perfectly united: that life so natural in its human virtue, so supernatural in its divine power: which has robbed death of its sting, and the grave of its victory, by faith in Him who 'was delivered for our offences and was raised again for our justification': which has ennobled and sanctified even the wants and weaknesses of our mortal nature, by the memory of Him who was anhungered in the wilderness and athirst upon the cross: who mourned over the destruction of Jerusalem and wept at the grave of Lazarus'.[1]

This passage could not fail to please Maurice, yet it did not content him. Inasmuch as Mansel was insisting on history and fact in contrast with metaphysical abstractions, Maurice could not but approve and admire. But a careful reading of the passage shows that Mansel treats the

[1] *Limits of Religious Thought*, pp. 106–7, and *What is Revelation?*, p. 349.

ncarnation as sanctioning the precepts of morality rather
han as disclosing the nature of God. The revelation in
Christ is still only the announcement of regulative truths,
nd regulative truths are not enough. If Maurice had
ressed the point, he might have urged that if Jesus
Christ gives us only regulative truths, if He reveals not
vhat God is, but what God is like, then the Arians were
ight who spoke of Jesus Christ as like God or as of like
ubstance with God. Mansel would not have accepted
his conclusion but his theory of regulative truths seems
o involve it.

'No man has ever seen God: the only Son, who is in
he bosom of the Father, he has made him known.'
Mansel so stressed the first clause that he seriously im-
aired the value of the second. Maurice rightly asserted
he reality of the knowledge of God that Christ has
rought.

CHAPTER VII

MAURICE ON EDUCATION

◈━━━◈

F. D. MAURICE was a born teacher and his interest in
and services to education were life-long. At the age of
twenty-three he was editing a short-lived educational
magazine. He took part in the discussions and contro
versies which attended the increase of the Government
grant to the modest sum of £30,000 and the establishment
of an Education Committee to administer the grant, which
committee later became the Board of Education. He
lived to share in the discussions and controversies which
accompanied Foster's Education Act of 1870.

In his early writings on education he was much under
the influence of Plato and he was among the first admirers
of Pestalozzi. He believed that the teaching of an
elementary subject like arithmetic was stultified by com
mercialism and could become an instrument of genuine
education only if we followed Plato in his appreciation of
number as the child's first acquaintance with abstract
ideas.

If arithmetic were taught properly to children, it would be
one of the most valuable instruments for cultivating their
faculties, for elucidating the perplexities which surround
them in a strange world, and for rescuing them from the
delusions of the senses. But in this shop-keeping country even
to hint at such an object as this is dangerous. To force a child
to learn by heart a multiplication table, of the meaning of
which it is utterly ignorant, to make it in its very cradle a

selfish calculator, to fit it for the pursuits of the world, and to make it unintelligent even in these pursuits—this is the end and effect of modern education.

The disciple of Plato who expressed himself on the subject of arithmetic thus grandiloquently at the age of twenty-three, at a later date could put his meaning more simply. 'To regard numbers with the kind of wonder with which a child regards them, to feel that when we are learning the laws of numbers we are looking into the very laws of the Universe, this makes the study of exceeding worth to the mind and character. Yet it need not create the least impatience of ordinary occupations. On the contrary it helps us to know that nothing is mean but what is false.'

Education is a spiritual concern and it will be ruined if it becomes the handmaid of commerce or is subject to political authority. So, in 1839, Maurice was opposed to the inspection of religious teaching and doubtful about the wisdom of voluntary societies in accepting State aid. He criticised Lord Melbourne's government unmercifully and unjustly. In his *Letters to a Quaker* (1838), he claimed that education was primarily the work of the Church. The duty of the State is simply this, to give the Church free scope to educate the people. In a later work, *The Representation and Education of the People* (1866), he reiterated his view that 'The Church must educate. A people cannot be educated aright by its political rulers or government.' The corruption of youth in totalitarian States tempts one to underline these judgments. If education were simply the imparting of information, then indeed it might be undertaken by the State. But this would not be true education and it would not make for national unity. Maurice thought a bread-and-butter education based on the three R's actually increased class division rather than promoted national unity.

If Maurice's insistence that education should be the work of the Church rather than of the State,[1] is a safeguard against the evils of totalitarianism, his insistence on education as the prime factor in national unity might seem to make in the other direction. Maurice was a fervent nationalist. Incidentally he much admired Mazzini. He interpreted Protestantism as a nation's protest against its nationality being ignored, which is perhaps the kindest interpretation one can put on 'Reformation after the manner of the Tudors'. But the work of education should be directed to giving the men of our day the sense that they belong to a people, that they have an inheritance from the past and a destiny in the future. The Nazis might say the same. But Maurice believed that true nationalism must be rooted in Old Testament feelings respecting the sacredness of a nation's life and history. And this sense of sacredness will never issue in the worship of the nation-state; it will be reflected in the conviction that the nation has been and may yet be the instrument of God's purposes. God's purposes cannot be equated with national aggrandisement. Though making this claim for the Church, Maurice recognised that the clergy are not qualified to conduct the education of the country. The teaching profession must be developed alongside the clerical profession and must be independent of it. But he claimed that teachers should be allowed and encouraged to start from a definite Christian basis for their

[1] Cf. his letter to Hort in 1870 (*Life and Letters*, II, 613): 'In time the Comtist doctrine of a distinction between the educating and the governing power must be recognised and that no power can be an educating one which does not appeal to the spirit of the child and the man.'

work. He did not believe in secular education and he was sceptical about undenominationalism. In the discussion of 1870, he defined two fundamental convictions which he felt he could not suppress in any teaching he undertook.

First, the bond which unites me to the Dissenter and to the Secularist is the conviction that God is their Father as well as mine, in a Son of Man, who is their Lord and mine. I cannot refuse to tell my children this. In so doing I should break the tie between me and those who differ from me. Second, the belief, that God is the Educator of men and children, is the only strength in which I feel that I can educate them. If I openly suppress this belief while I hold it, I shall be really talking Religion under the guise of Secularism; for it is part of my very being: it must come out somehow. Or if I outwardly and inwardly suppress these beliefs that I may meet your requirements I become merely a machine for conveying certain scraps of information, not a living teacher at all.[1]

Clearly Maurice himself could never suppress such convictions. They coloured all his life and teaching. But one cannot guarantee that all teachers will adopt these convictions as their basis. Maurice would not have advocated credal tests for teachers. So far as he envisaged the problem, he would have pinned his faith to the Training Colleges. Offer intending teachers the best training you can give them and then trust them to make the best use of it. By 1870 Maurice realised that the State would have to take larger responsibilities, especially larger financial responsibilities, in the field of education. I think he would not have wished to eliminate the dual system. Certainly he would have viewed with apprehension anything in the nature of a State monopoly in education. I do not think he would have objected to the

[1] *Life*, ii, 611.

work of His Majesty's Inspectors, and he would have approved the development of agreed syllabuses of religious instruction, but the essential for education is to secure the integrity and independence of the teacher. He criticised University education as being too much a repetition of grammar-school studies. In his three-volume novel, *Eustace Conway*, he condemned the remote dry-as-dust character of University studies, in a paragraph which was quoted with approval by John Stuart Mill in his dissertation on civilization. Reform of the Universities by statute might be necessary. But the Universities ought not to be adapted to the tastes and notions of the public. They should correct and expand the public mind, not stoop to it. Perhaps no principle needs to be more jealously guarded to-day.

Maurice's most signal services to the cause of higher education are connected with the founding of Queen's College in 1848 and of the Working Men's College in 1854. In both enterprises he was the leading spirit. The first started as a very modest contribution to the training of governesses, at a time when governesses were expected to know and teach everything and often did in fact know little or nothing. Family misfortune often drove girls to undertake the work of governess, though they might have no aptitude for it and no real education. So Queen's College was founded to enable young women to fit themselves for this calling. In his opening address Maurice set out to raise the governess' standard of self-respect. Education, the training of an immortal spirit, ought not to be undertaken lightly as one undertakes, let us say, the selling of ribbons. The vocation of a teacher is an awful one, in the true sense of the term 'awful'. A teacher should think highly of his or her job, and claim respect for a great calling. 'The College which thus began with the special object of improving the status of governesses, proved to be the first step towards a general improvement in the education of women.' At the end of its first year, its classes were thrown open to students who were not committed to becoming governesses. The age-limit for admission was put at twelve years of age, so that the larger junior side of the College was in effect a Girls' High School. The College had no endowments to start with. It enjoyed the Queen's patronage and it was granted a royal charter in 1853, but its success depended on the unselfish devotion and energy of its founders. Maurice and other members of the King's College staff gave of their best to the College. Maurice himself was Principal from 1848 to 1854. He was Professor of History and Theology during the same period and after a break, due partly to his disapproval of a change in the constitution of the governing body and partly to the demands of the new undertaking in the Working Men's College, he returned to the staff as Professor from 1858 till he moved to Cambridge in 1866. He made a profound impression on the minds of many who became leaders in the higher education of girls and women. The founder of Girton College, Cambridge, Miss Emily Davies, and great head-mistresses like Miss Buss and Miss Beale, were wholly or in part educated at Queen's College and may well be supposed to have received within its walls the impulse that made them, in different directions, such earnest reformers of women's education. The inspiration, then, both of Cheltenham and of Girton derives in no small degree from Maurice.

Valuable as were Maurice's services to the higher education of women, his outstanding contribution to

F. D. MAURICE

progress in the realm of education will always be found in
his association with the Working Men's College. His
interest in the problems of education for the workers
antedates the founding of the College by many years. In
1842, through Julius Hare, he got into touch with Daniel
Macmillan, one of two brothers who founded the well-
known publishing firm of that name. Daniel Macmillan
was convinced that the workers wanted better intellectual
and spiritual guidance than they were getting. He believed
that men like Hare and Maurice could provide it. He put
his concern in a letter addressed to Hare.

One [he says] who [like himself] has attended some of their
religious and political meetings, the Chartist meetings, and
Socialist meetings; who has heard them speak; has learnt
what the hard-working men among them are really moving
after; who knows how they often laugh at the ineptitudes of
the public spouters who pretend to lead them; who knows
how very sensibly they (these hard-working men) sometimes talk; how little faith they have in all existing churches
and spiritual guides; how very ignorant they are of the real
opinions and designs of Churchmen; one who really knows
these things and does not trust to newspaper reporters or to the
facts and generalisations of *Edinburgh* and *Quarterly Review*
writers, must see that there is no spiritual guidance in existence at all equal to the wants of our time. . . . What are called
religious tracts don't answer the purpose; they may confirm
those who already believe them, but never reach the masses of
the poor in and about London and other large towns.[1]

He described the papers they were actually reading, and
appealed to Hare and Maurice to endeavour to reach
these men. He said that the books of each of them had
shown that they could reach this class. Nothing much

[1] Cf. *Life*, I, 329.

came of this at the time. The spread of Owenism and of Chartism seemed, however, to call for some propaganda on other lines. The crisis of 1848 led Kingsley and Maurice to issue *Politics for the People*, and to embark on the Christian Socialist crusade, of which I shall have more to say in the following chapter. Tracts on Christian Socialism began to appear in 1850 and the first productive profit-sharing co-operatives were started. But the productive co-operatives initiated by the Christian Socialists hung fire, whereas the co-operative stores started by the Rochdale pioneers in 1844 were making steady progress. Maurice became convinced that the workers must take the initiative in co-operative undertakings. Rochdale succeeds where the Christian Socialists fail. But in any case co-operation must be backed by education. The productive enterprises foundered on the rocks of ignorance and prejudice. Maurice felt more and more certain that it was in the field of education that intellectuals could be of most help to the workers. He claimed, as he said, 'for those who call themselves the educated classes of England at least the privilege and the right of helping the manual workers to educate themselves'. When he was deprived of his chair at King's College, he threw himself into the project of founding a Working Men's College. In June and July 1854, to arouse interest and to raise money, Maurice delivered six lectures which were published under the title *Learning and Working*. He was so far successful in both objects that the College was opened in the following November in Red Lion Square.

When Westcott was asked by his daughter to recommend to her a book on the subject of education, he unhesitatingly selected Maurice's *Learning and Working*. It is certainly a classic on adult education and might well find a

place beside Newman's *Idea of a University* and Sir Richard
Livingstone's *Future in Education* on the bookshelves of
every W.E.A. tutor. It is an admirable introduction to
the problems of scope and method in adult education.

Maurice begins the course by defending what may seem
a paradox, this namely that in the strict sense adult learning is primary education. Historically, adult learning
precedes juvenile learning. He brings forward a number
of instances from medieval history to show that the
education of an illiterate nation does normally begin with
adults. The campaigns to overcome illiteracy in many
countries to-day lend support to Maurice's contention. I
think he might share the view of some critics that adult
education has not received adequate attention in the
latest Education Act. But the over-elaborated historical
illustrations of his thesis need not detain us. What is more
important is the implied principle. Why should we try to
persuade adult members of the community to take continued education seriously? Because only so shall we get
the full benefit of education of the young and the
adolescent. Possibly the most successful parish priest in
the north of London in my father's time was the Rev.
J. E. Watts Ditchfield, who subsequently became Bishop
of Chelmsford. He concentrated on his men's meeting
which at its peak had some 800 members. He argued
that if he got the men, he would get the women and
children too. And he did. So Maurice argued, we must
convince working men of their need of education and
provide for them the education they need. If the men
become interested, we shall get the women.

If I did not believe that the education of working men would
lead us by the most direct road to the education of working
women, I should care much less for it. But I am sure that the

earnest thoughtful man who is also a labourer with his hands, instead of grudging his wife the best culture she can obtain, will demand that she shall have it. He will long to have a true household, he will desire to bring up brave citizens. He will understand that his country looks to the wives and mothers, in every one of her classes, as the best security that the next generation of Englishmen shall not make her ashamed.

Somewhat similarly, if children's education is to prosper parents must be keen, not just keen on their children's education, but keen on education for its own sake and for themselves. So far as our national education fails, it fails largely because school and home pull different ways. Mr Mallon has wittily suggested that as a solution for the problem of Germany, the school-leaving age in that country should be raised to seventy-five! The policy would pay in England as well as in Germany. Education must become a life-long interest and a life-long process.

The second lecture discusses learning and leisure. Maurice is arguing that learning is more readily associated with work than with leisure and with experience than with immaturity. One might conclude that adult workers should be in a favourable position for acquiring learning. Education in schools and colleges is apt to be too bookish, too much divorced from practical activities and real life. For most men, perhaps for all men, their powers of appreciation are best developed by practice and experience. From this standpoint Maurice offers us a highly appreciative estimate of industrial schools. However narrow and selfish the aims of their promoters, such schools may have a real advantage over grammar schools. The agreed opinion in favour of industrial schools which Maurice reports is only now coming into its own. The passage in which he outlines the case is worth recalling at some length.

I have heard that some who have spent their lives in promoting the instruction of the poor, and whose purses are as open as they ever were, have declared that they will not give a shilling to any school in which work and teaching are not combined. Now, though I am sure that one of their objects is to prepare the children for being tailors or shoemakers or cooks or housemaids hereafter, I cannot believe that this is their chief object. Sullen masters and mistresses may say that they do not care for the school apprenticeship, that they could teach their servants better themselves. But the advantages of this discipline are found to be immediate, not prospective. The children may not at once earn better wages in consequence of the facility they have acquired, but they do their school tasks infinitely better. Not only are their bodily powers cultivated, but the words which they read acquire a life and reality which they scarcely ever have when the book stands by itself, when the only business is to spell it out. On the other hand, the work, even if it is imperfectly executed, is understood to be part of the day's duties; its character is raised; and the child does not look forward to the workshop as something which is to separate him from all that he is doing before he goes to it.[1]

Maurice goes on to argue that leisure is possibly less favourable to learning than work. Work and learning have no natural antipathy to one another. They readily join forces. But leisure will often betray learning. 'The question has been greatly discussed in our day, "If a man will not work, neither let him eat" and under what limitations it is applicable to us. There is a more terrible sentence still, of which we should seek diligently to avert the execution upon ourselves and upon those who have

[1] *Learning and Working*, pp. 47 ff.

all they need of outward consolations—"If a man will not work, neither let him think.'"

The third lecture is entitled, 'Learning and Money Worship incompatible.' Maurice has argued that there is a natural affinity between learning and work, but clearly this depends on the character of work and the spirit in which it is undertaken. He perceived very clearly that 'we must raise Work to make it fit for association with Learning as well as bring Learning to bear upon Work'. And daily work has degenerated because of the disease of Mammon-worship. Here I must reproduce a page or two which give expression to Maurice's indictment of the rapidly developing competitive industrialism and profit-seeking commercialism.

If steady work is favourable to Education, unsteady work— gambling work (it is almost profaneness to join two such words together)—must be the most fatal obstacle to it. And the truth must be spoken. We are becoming a nation of gamblers. Life is beginning to be regarded as a shuffling of cards, as a throwing of dice. We do not ask what we are to do, but what is likely to turn up, if we make such and such a cast. Handicrafts, Trades, Professions, are to be undertaken upon a calculation of chances, not from the sense of a vocation. How can we think quietly, how can we pursue science, which only converses with that which *is*, while our whole minds are busy with possibilities and contingencies?

I state the case in this way, because I wish you earnestly to reflect, 1st. That precisely the same disease which is affecting the working class, is affecting all classes; 2nd. That the disease has its roots in a habit of mind, which is communicated from the higher classes to the working class; 3rd. That there is no way so effectual of restoring the whole of society to its right tone, as by doing what in us lies for the reformation of this portion of it.

If you take care that the notion shall be checked among all over whom you have influence, that Money is the measure of worth; that professions exist for the sake of the Money which they bring in; that the acquisition and the accumulation of it is the purpose for which men are to live and die, you will be laying your axe to the root of an evil from which the best sumptuary regulations can only cut off a few branches, if they do not, as is sometimes the case, promote its growth.[1]

If Leisure does not necessarily favour Learning, Rest in the sense of a feeling of security in one's daily work and a proper alternation of work and relaxation is indispensable to Learning. Hence the importance of shorter hours of labour and the checking of overtime. And be it remembered, Work must be so organised and so motived that it makes real education possible for working men. Maurice tells us that there were frequent complaints that the lectures in the Mechanics' Institutes rather graze the surface of men's minds than penetrate into them. Popular adult education tended to become a form of entertainment or diversion. But the worker is not merely entitled to receive certain crumbs of knowledge which fall from the rich man's table, to a scrap here and there of irregular disjointed learning, which is rather a burden to his spirit than a power to raise it. 'He is intended to share with you [the educated classes] the deepest and most universal part of your treasures, those which belong not to classes but to men. [These treasures must be dispensed] regularly and methodically as if they were portions of our common food which must be received and which belong to the life of all.'[2] Maurice doubted whether any class would retain the deepest and most universal part of our cultural inheri-

---

[1] *Learning and Working*, pp. 86–7.
[2] Ibid. p. 97.

tance unless it was shared with members of every other class.[1] 'The whole country must look for its blessings through the elevation of the working class. We must all sink if it is not raised.'[2]

A change in the organisation and spirit of industry and commerce is essential if the aims of adult education are to be achieved. But Maurice did not regard the adult education movement, as some have done, as primarily the acquisition of knowledge for the sake of obtaining political power. Knowledge is no doubt power, but to concentrate on this consideration and to persuade men to study with a view to obtaining political power is to degrade learning. In a New Year's address at the College in 1863, Maurice spoke of acquisition and illumination. While he did not condemn talk about acquiring and transmitting knowledge, such talk makes us think of knowledge much as we think of property, or money. The acquisition of knowledge is apt to become division. But if we recall that learning is illumination and that knowledge comes to us as light does, then we shall find how truly knowledge is an unveiling of that which is and of that which is common.[3] 'Commonplaces are more worthy to be thought of than rarities. The secrets of our life lie hid in them. Never, therefore, slight them.'[4] The right approach to any subject of study depends on our putting illumination before acquisition. Logic will be primarily the study of how to think. 'Here, as elsewhere, we are engaged about that which is common to human beings; we are learning not what some may do and others not, but what must be true about all.' If logic be looked upon as a mere acquirement, it may be either

---

[1] Cf. *Learning and Working*, p. vii, 169–70.   [2] Ibid. p. vii.
[3] *Friendship of Books*, p. 346.   [4] Ibid. p. 348.

child's play or sophistry, a scheme for imposing upon plain men. 'If it is looked upon as a discovery of laws which we are all meant to obey, it may often save us from wasting our time in child's play, it may be a protection against many impostures.' This was always Maurice's attitude. Learning is always concerned with our common humanity. It is prostituted if it is regarded as a weapon in class-conflict or as a source of individual self-aggrandisement.

Maurice, in his course of lectures, turned next to the bearing of education on the maintenance of freedom and order. We are preoccupied to-day with the problem of planning without sacrificing liberty. Behind the particular problem of the present time lie deep-seated cravings for freedom and order and the constant tension between them. A true education will at once stimulate and satisfy these cravings. But it must be a true education. Here he found himself opposed to the secularists who ignore or depreciate the spiritual nature of man, as well as to the anti-secularists who would keep science in theological leading-strings. His conclusion on this point needs to be constantly remembered.

I must disclaim all intention of fashioning an eclectical scheme of education which shall be half secular, half religious. Against this kind of compound I would most earnestly protest. I believe it must be powerless for good to any class, but utterly and demonstrably powerless for the working classes. There is a kind of Christianised teaching about philology, history, physiology, which seems to me most unchristian. It is offensive to the scientific man, because it twists facts to a moral: to the devout man because it treats the laws of God's universe and His acts as less sacred than our inferences from them: to the working man, because he asks us to help him to see the truth of things, and he thinks we are plotting to deceive him. If you regard Christianity as something which is to be spread and sprinkled over the surface of things, to prevent truth from being dangerous—if you have not courage to look into the roots of knowledge and science, because you are sure that the God of truth and righteousness is there,—you had better leave the working man alone, unless you desire to make him a thousand times more of an infidel than you give him credit for being already.[1]

If then we wish to give men Freedom and Order, what sort of curriculum should we draw up and what methods should we employ? With regard to method, the difference between the adult and the child must never be forgotten.

I have to remark, once for all, that we never can teach men as we teach boys, let their previous deficiencies be what they may...we feel instinctively that a man has rights, has a knowledge, has a position, which must be taken for granted and respected: that he must under no circumstances be put on a first form, and turned into a child. You cannot do it: you have no business to attempt it. The world has been teaching him—I must add with all reverence, God has been teaching him—whatever you have been doing. To overlook that fact, is simply to deprive yourself of the best opportunity of delivering him from the ignorance which cleaves to him.[2]

The method of adult education must be that of free discussion in an atmosphere of confidence and comradeship.

With regard to choice of subjects, Maurice believed a Working Men's College should offer a very wide choice indeed. The same will apply to the programme of a W.E.A., or an adult school movement or the extra-mural

[1] *Learning and Working*, p. 125.
[2] See p. 139. The detailed description of Maurice's conduct of Bible classes, given in his *Life and Letters*, i, 488–93, may well be studied as a model in the technique of adult education.

department of a University. You must be prepared to start with an adult student where his interest happens to be keenest at the moment and you must relate the study of any subject to his actual experience and his daily concerns. We cannot indeed lay it down that learning like charity must begin at home. Naturally, interest is likely to start with immediate surroundings, but if the eyes of the student happen to be directed to the heavens or the ends of the earth, let us start from some circumferential interest and work towards a domestic centre.

More important was Maurice's deliberate departure from a self-denying ordinance adopted by the Mechanics' Institutes. They excluded Politics and Religion as being controversial subjects. Maurice included both because they were controversial. Controversial subjects are those in which men are most keenly interested, and on which the illumination of true learning is most needed. I shall illustrate his views on the teaching of politics and theology, by some extracts which will be better than any summary or comment of my own.

On the place of politics in adult education he says: 'An education such as I am proposing for men, will fail of its object if it does not teach Politics.' As to method, the wisdom contained in a couple of pages can hardly be surpassed and is certainly not antiquated.

To make our working people aware of the treasures which they possess in the history of the country, I would begin with the topics that are most occupying us in this day. No doubt these are party topics—that is to say, each party in the country has its own views upon them. You may make that an excuse for passing them by, and for talking upon some subject upon which all people agree, or seem to agree. You may say, 'There is a Tory tradition about this point, and a Whig tradition. I find these working people rather impatient of both, inclined to take up with some Radical opinion which they fancy is not traditional. It is much better to move the 'previous question, and discourse of air-pumps and gases.' What is the effect? The most active and energetic thoughts of the minds with which you have to deal, are those which you do not meet, which you leave to the sport of any chance influence. You say to the most vigorous man, 'Your vigour is in our way; we had rather you were stupid or asleep; and we will try to find some part of you which is not alive, that we may address ourselves to that.' It would be better to take any course, even what I should think the narrowest, than this. Give them your Tory traditions or your Whig traditions; enforce them by the most passionate declamation, by the most one-sided exhibition of facts. Bring up your fierce Radicalism to confound both. In any of these ways you will do something; you will often irritate the man's faith, you will often outrage his conscience; perhaps you will find that you are not dealing very fairly with your own; but at least you will kindle some emotions, with which good will mix as well as evil. You will not leave the man to the thought which is the worst of all for him and for you, that there is nothing common between him and you; that you do not care for the same things, that you are indifferent whether you are fellow-citizens, or deadly foes.

I believe, indeed, that there is a more excellent way than either—one which those who care to educate working men and to educate thinking men, more than to propagate their opinions, will find. I believe that they will be able to point out the great and precious principles which have been vindicated by the Tory traditions and by the Whig traditions; the grievous loss which it would have been if either had been wanting to the land; the great and noble spirit which has gone forth in support of both. I believe that in justifying these, and in showing how, while apparently counteracting each other, they have nobly worked together for building up the nation, you would be able to point out far more clearly what have been the sins into which each party has fallen, and what reason each has afforded for the bitter complaints against it. You would then be able to explain, while confessing the good of both, while proving that good to be necessary for our time as well as for any past time, that there is a good which neither could effect, nor both together, and which we may effect if we profit by the wisdom of both, while we refuse to be bound by the exclusiveness of either. Thus a teacher may give the most cordial welcome to the convictions and hopes which he will find stirring in the hearts of the working men, and yet may bring the experience of history to remove their prejudices and diminish their asperities. This cannot be, if we do not come to the task with a willingness to have our own theories broken to pieces by facts; desirous to find men, better than we have supposed them to be; determined that what is right and true must be mightier and must show itself to be mightier than we and all other men are. This willing-ness, this determination, may grow weaker or firmer by practice. Nothing is so likely to weaken them as the habit of attacking others and apologising for ourselves. Nothing is so likely to strengthen them as the habit of bringing our thoughts into collision with those of men whom we wish to help, who will not take what we say for granted, who will often surprise us by their ignorance, often by showing us that they have got beyond our depth.[1]

The case for including Theology is similar to that for teaching Politics. Maurice states it thus:

Unless I felt sure that the working men were divines in embryo as well as logicians in embryo—in other words, that they must think about Divinity, whether we speak to them of it or not: unless I believed that their vague thoughts about it interfere with the feeling that they are men and have the

[1] *Learning and Working*, pp. 141-3.

rights of men—and that it is possible to give their thoughts harmony, and so to do more for the freedom and the order of their minds than by any other of our lessons; I should rather avoid a subject which no man of common sense or ordinary experience hopes to handle without giving offence. Having that conviction very strongly and deeply rooted in my mind, so strongly that it must have its expression in every lesson of mine on any subject, if it did not find this direct outlet, I think it would be dishonest to the working people if I did not give them notice of it, by using a word which is likely to frighten many of them. Of course no one need take more of our instruction than he likes; but he has a right to know what sort of people they are who offer it; he has cause to complain if they sail under false colours. If I asked any one to suppress his convictions, I should feel as if I were under a sort of obligation to stifle my own: but as I think all peril to truth as well as charity lies in evasions and concealments—and that there will be most safety, and most tenderness of others, when every one speaks out that which is deepest in him—I must exercise the privilege of which I count it a shame and a folly that we should deprive any. And as I make that our defence for giving a substantive place to Theology in our College course, so it is upon this principle that I should wish to see it taught. There are those who suppose that if we excite any one to tell that which makes him discontented with us and our conclusions, we must be propagating doubts and divisions. I can only say that I have tried, and I believe it to be the best method of delivering our pupils and ourselves from doubts and divisions, of leading them and us to know where we are standing, and what we have to stand upon. If I believed that Truth belonged to us and that we could settle strifes, I should think and act otherwise. Believing that Truth is of God, and that our divisions come from our narrow and partial apprehensions of it, I would ask Him to vindicate it, and to establish Unity in His own way. If I thought that we could give men Freedom or Order, I should leave the science of Theology alone; I should suppose that no such science existed. I would teach it, because I believe that God desires Freedom and Order for us, and will help us to desire them and claim them for ourselves.[1]

It will be remembered that Maurice had discovered along with Thomas Erskine that life should be regarded as a process of education rather than as a time of probation. God is the educator of men. Through every avenue of their experience, He is teaching His children Himself. The task then of the Christian educator is to help his fellow pupils in God's school to realise where they are. Maurice, like George Fox, had been commissioned to turn men to their inward teacher.

[1] *Learning and Working*, pp. 156-8.

CHAPTER VIII

MAURICE AND SOCIAL ETHICS

SOCIALLY, the early decades of the nineteenth century form one of the grimmest periods in our history as a people. The costs both of a prolonged and exhausting war, and of far-reaching revolutions in industry and agriculture were borne in the main by the common people and issued in the degrading poverty which has so long disgraced our urban civilisation. At the same time, it must be recognised that the enclosure movement which deprived the agricultural labourer of his modest share in the land and the inventions which rendered obsolete the domestic crafts and industries, produced the wealth which sustained a rapidly expanding population. At the beginning of the revolutionary period neither Church nor State was equipped to deal with the new conditions. The parochial and diocesan organisation of the Church could not cope with the new aggregation of population in mining and industrial areas. If Wesley had not ignored parochial considerations, the sheep would have remained without a shepherd in many centres. The State was governed by political parties and by a parliament, which were increasingly unrepresentative of the people at large. The Poor Law had broken down. Local government was in urgent need of reform. The Law depended on savage penalties. There was no equivalent to our modern police force. Popular education had hardly begun. The abuse of child-labour was unrestrained. The problem of intemperance associated with the introduction of spirits in the eighteenth century had not been seriously faced and certainly not solved. Intense poverty and widespread unrest marked the period that followed the close of the Napoleonic wars. In this period Maurice grew to manhood.

We get a glimpse of the situation and of its impact on his mind in a letter from his mother describing the Bristol riots of 1830.

I cannot but think that this rising of the people, these midnight fires, have been very necessary to awaken us to a sense of the dreadful sin of poor labourers having been for many years obliged to work hard for scarcely wages enough to buy them potatoes. It was proved at one meeting that a *noble* lord's workmen were employed in hedging and ditching for *two shillings a week*, and the parish paid them three more! Five shillings a week to support himself, wife and children. Every demand that the poor creatures have made has been most reasonable. I have not heard of one that has demanded for the labourers more than 2/- or 2/3 a day, and how they can do with that is wonderful....High time for something dreadful to rouse persons from such wickedness. We have had sermons here for the times. Mr Betheridge advertised one here on Sunday morning, in which he endeavoured to prove that Sabbath-breaking was the sin that occasioned these awful visitations. Surely there was little wisdom in speaking only of this sin. Though we have many crying and dreadful national sins, yet the obvious one pointed out at this moment is that the hire of the labourer is withheld: but the farmers say they cannot pay more unless rent and tithes are reduced. I trust this will be the case, and that it will soon be a fixed and established rule that the poor shall be well paid.

Maurice shared his mother's sympathies and his mother's judgment. But it was not until the crisis of 1848 that he found his positive contribution to the cause of the common people. He was not satisfied with any of the reform movements, which bulked large at the beginning of the Victorian era.

He shared in large measure the reaction from the French Revolution, and he was much under the influence of Edmund Burke, though he distrusted Burke's reliance on prejudice. But Burke's exposure of the doctrinaire character of the principles of the French Revolution appealed to Maurice, and revolutionary violence was abhorrent to him. His strong sense of the value of national characteristics made him distrust assertions about the Rights of Man. It was de Maistre who said he had met Frenchmen, Germans, Italians but had never met Man, with a capital M. Maurice would have sympathised with him, though he had a firmer hold than de Maistre on our common humanity.

The French Revolution had shown that social progress cannot be secured by ignoring nationality, by disparaging history, or by suppressing religion in the name of Reason. But reform in England was not likely to ape French models. When Maurice was at Cambridge, the star of Jeremy Bentham was already in the ascendant. The reformers of his day were disciples of the philosophical radicals, learning utilitarianism in ethics from Bentham and the Mills, and economic theory from Adam Smith and Ricardo. From his Cambridge days onwards, Maurice joined issue with the Benthamites. They seemed to him to start from an atomic individualism, which to him was utterly distasteful. The individual is the embodiment of pure egotism, and if on any occasion he acts in an altruistic or disinterested manner, it must be attributed to enlightened self-interest. Maurice caricatured this supposed principle of the Bentham School in one of the characters in his novel, who justifies the abduction of a lady and the betrayal of a friend on strict utilitarian principles. It is legitimate to suggest that the enlightened pursuit of self-interest might be held to justify the abduction of a rich Quaker heiress, and one might argue that such conduct would promote the greatest happiness of the greatest number. But presumably no Utilitarian ever did argue and act in this fashion. To suggest that they frequently did so would be libel. In the Bentham school, this individualism led on to the assertion of the equality of human beings before the law. The individual was normally the best judge of his own interests, and should be left to pursue happiness in his own way. So the Utilitarians furthered the cause of political and economic liberty. When they realised that individuals constantly misjudge their real interests, education was the remedy—education must enlighten self-interest. But Halévy, who has given us such a masterly study of the philosophical radicals, brings out a curious contradiction in their attitude towards legal reform and their attitude towards Government action in the economic sphere. In political and social life, it was recognised that the interests of individuals and of groups may conflict. The pursuit of happiness by A may diminish or destroy the happiness of B. To ensure a harmony of interests, legal restraint will be necessary. The duty of Government is to establish such a harmony or some approximation to it. But in industry and commerce it is assumed that if each pursues his own interest energetically, he will promote the common good. Help yourself and you help society. There is a natural harmony of economic interests, which will establish itself if Government will only stand aside.

Laissez-faire radicalism was on the top of the wave in the middle of the century. We have moved so far and so fast from this outlook that it is difficult to realise its strength and its attraction. Actual interventions of Government to restrain or direct trade were at the time almost purely mischievous. The claims for private enterprise were not ill-founded. Dr Smiles's *Self-Help* had a well-deserved vogue. The economic interests of individuals or classes do not conflict necessarily and all the time. Exchange is no robbery and should normally be beneficial to both parties to the transaction. At the same time the optimism of the *laissez-faire* radicals was a strange illusion. Men needed the rude shock of the insistence of Karl Marx on the reality of the conflict of class-interests before they awoke from their dream. When James Martineau began his ministry at Hope Street, Liverpool, in 1849, he tells us that 'he was surprised at the way in which English Society had run after the "Gospel of the Economists" which cries out "Let a man help himself." "Help yourself" was the modern gospel of England. "Help one another" was the ancient gospel of the Christian Church.' Maurice would have endorsed this verdict. It is curious to recall that in 1836 he was nominated for the chair of political economy in the University of Oxford and for a brief space had the backing of some of the leaders of the Oxford Movement. The other and eventually successful candidate was Merivale. Both candidates were similarly qualified for the post since neither knew anything of the science they proposed to teach. Maurice certainly had not grasped the analysis of the rationale of economic activity which we owe to the classical economists, but he did know that 'Help yourself' is not an adequate gospel; he did know that co-operation rather than competition, should dominate industry; he did know that self-interest, however enlightened, is not enough. He did not dwell so much as others did on the need for Government intervention to protect child-labour or to shorten hours, though he welcomed such social legislation. He was more concerned about helping the workers to help themselves. It was Ludlow who had spent much of his time and obtained much of his education in France, who drew Maurice's attention to some social projects in that country. In particular Ludlow told him of Fourier's phalansteries—self-maintaining industrial communities. The experiments of Maurice and his friends were not so ambitious as Fourier's proposals. But they were based on the belief that the workers could do more to raise their standard of living by co-operation than by strikes to raise wages. Maurice thought the co-operative movement might do more for the working classes than the Trade Union movement. I think he would have been interested in the discovery that if the Miners' Federation had invested in the mines the money spent in strike-pay during the last generation, they might by now be in possession of the mines and in a position to reorganise them to their hearts' content. This is not so simple as it sounds, but more might have been done by constructive measures than by industrial conflict. But the Christian Socialist group associated with Maurice was largely instrumental in securing legal recognition and legal protection for both Co-operative Societies and Trade Unions. Their propaganda on behalf of the co-operative movement was embodied in a series of tracts on Christian Socialism. Maurice explains the choice and meaning of the term 'Christian Socialism' in a letter to Ludlow.

I see it clearly. We must not beat about the bush. What right have we to address the English people? We must have something special to tell them, or we ought not to speak. 'Tracts on Christian Socialism' is, it seems to me, the only title which will define our object, and will commit us at once to the conflict we must engage in sooner or later with the unsocial Christians and the unchristian Socialists. It is a great thing not to leave people to poke out our object and proclaim it with infinite triumph. 'Why, you are Socialists in disguise.' 'In disguise, not a bit of it. There it is staring you in the face upon the title page!' 'You want to thrust in ever so much priestcraft under a good revolutionary name.' 'Well, did not we warn you of it? Did we not profess that our intended something was quite different from what your Owenish lectures meant?' This is the fair play which English people like, and which will save us from a number of long prefaces, paraphrases, apologetical statements which waste time when one wants to be getting to business.

What is clear is that Christian Socialism, as Maurice and his friends understood it, is bound up with co-operation rather than with collectivism, with profit-sharing and co-partnership rather than with common-ownership. The Christian Socialists were not committed to any particular scheme of economic organisation. They thought things should be subordinate to persons and that wealth should subserve welfare and they looked to the working classes to bring this to pass.

If Maurice was opposed to the economics of *laissez-faire* and self-help, he was equally dissatisfied with Benthamism in politics. The sovereignty of the people, whether based on Rousseau's 'Social Contract' or on Bentham's slogan 'the greatest happiness of the greatest number' got no support from Maurice. Bentham may have stripped off all the romance which early enthusiasm attached to the principles of the French Revolution, but his more sober rationalism comes to the same thing in the end. 'The greatest happiness of the greatest number—the will of the majority—these were the formulas under which all ideas of society and government were comprehended: What could not be reduced to them must be fiction.' But Bentham was as indifferent to history as the French revolutionaries. If in substituting sober rationalism for romance he did homage to the habits and instincts of the English citizen, yet it was not only romance that disappeared in his hands. 'The old English belief that the life of a people is a continuous life—the dream of a nation as anything but the sum of its inhabitants at any given time—was also scattered to the winds.' Bentham won his way by his grip on detail. He showed himself a practical reformer and the English will always listen to a practical man. Thus France (through Bentham) had won a singular triumph. The idea of the sovereignty of the people—that is to say, of the greatest number—had vanquished that class of Englishmen which cared least about ideas. The progress of this idea of the sovereignty of the people seemed to Maurice as dangerous as it seemed to Burke. Indeed, somewhere he echoes Burke's phrase about the people having no right to cashier their monarch. He believed that the monarchy and aristocracy had a rightful place in an organised Christian society and that authority was not derived from the people. While he would have the people represented in Parliament, he had grave misgivings about democracy as a principle and as a form of government. This came out in a curious episode connected with the Christian Socialist Tracts. In 1852 Lord Goderich submitted the manuscript of a pamphlet on 'the Duty of the Age' for inclusion in the series. Tom

Hughes accepted it, read it and was delighted with it, and since Maurice was not available to pass judgment on it, he sent it down to Kingsley for his opinion. Describing the incident Hughes wrote to Maurice's son, 'I received the tract back from Kingsley with a perfect song of triumph, that a young lord should at last have taken his place frankly in the front line of the people's army.' Hughes had the tract set up in type. 'I ordered it to be printed on good paper with ample margin—and put upon the title-page my two favourite quotations, and we all thought millennium was a coming with a wet sail! When lo! and behold your father turns up, and I, in gayness of heart, wrote to obtain his sanction to publication, just as a matter of form. I got in reply a precious wigging (the only one I ever had) with orders to suppress the whole edition.' Lord Goderich had declared himself a democrat and Maurice would have none of it.

This suspicion of democracy was shared by many, who were by no means Die-Hard Tories. Thus Baldwin Brown, in a sympathetic exposition of democracy, goes out of his way to dissociate himself from the democratic standpoint. He explains that democracy is the reversal of feudalism, that the democratic order arranges itself round the sovereign people. The supreme question is their good. It asserts that property is a privilege conferred by society and modified by society. Baldwin Brown adds that 'there is something indefensible in present absolute ownership of large estates (*let me say this who am no democrat* but am simply doing my best to put fairly the democratic point of view)'. Martineau similarly disclaimed the title 'democrat'. This attitude towards democracy may be illustrated further by an observation of Stopford Brooke on the death of Palmerston in 1865. 'He (Palmerston) was the great

barrier against the next great stride of Democracy.'
Stopford Brooke anticipates measures likely to revolu-
tionise England and foresees a time when Liberals like
himself will have apparently to adopt Conservative views
to check as far as possible the eagerness of Reformers
who will run in blind enthusiasm into the arms of
Revolutionists.

On what did these doubts about democracy rest?
Clearly on its levelling and equalitarian tendencies. De
Tocqueville's analysis of the tendencies of American
democracy made a great impression on the mind of
Victorian England. Inge in his sketch of the Victorian
Age quotes Sybel as saying, 'Universal Suffrage has
always heralded the end of parliamentary government'.
(Presumably the plebiscite which made Louis Napoleon
Emperor in 1851 was the nearest example.) De Tocqueville caps this by saying that the more successful a democracy is in levelling a population, the less will be the
resistance which the next despotism will encounter. This
was Maurice's view also. 'Reconstitute society upon the
democratic basis—treat the sovereign and the aristocracy
as not intended to rule and guide the land, as only holding
their commissions from us—and I anticipate nothing but a
most accursed sacerdotal rule or a military despotism
with the great body of the population in either case
morally, politically, physically serfs, more than they are at
present or have ever been.'

Maurice was also well aware that majority rule may
itself become a form of tyranny. Mill, in his essay on
Bentham, says, 'The power of the majority is salutary so
far as it is used defensively, not offensively—as its exertion
is tempered by respect for the personality of the individual
and deference to the superiority of cultivated intelligence.'

Maurice would have said amen to this, except that he would have stressed reverence for truth and the moral law rather than deference to high-brows! But he detected in democracy a tendency to flatter king Demos.

Whoever flatters a mob—I would say this emphatically on the eve of a general election [1866]—does not reverence a people, does not love them, but hates them and despises them. With this flattery I would join the boast of conforming to the will of a majority. So help me God, I do not mean to follow the will of a majority, I hope never to follow it, always to set it at nought. And for that expression about 'the greatest happiness for the greatest number', I do not understand it. I have no measure of it. I cannot tell what happiness is, or how it is to be distributed among the greatest number, or how the greatest number is to be ascertained. If it could be put to the vote of the greatest number what they could have for happiness, I have no security that they will not decide for something profoundly low and swinish.[1]

Again, Maurice perceived as clearly as J. S. Mill that the complete dominance of any class in society is an evil. Mill wrote 'whenever any variety of human nature becomes preponderant in a community, it imposes upon all the rest of society its own type: forcing all, either to submit to it or to imitate it'.[2] Maurice touches on this danger when he says, 'When thoughtful men say that a working age of the world is about to begin, they mean,

---

[1] *Representation and Education*, pp. 201–2.
[2] Compare with Mill's judgment this passage from John Nichol's book on Carlyle (p. 212): 'Events are every day demonstrating the fallacy of his (Carlyle's) view of democracy as the embodiment of *laissez-faire*. Kant, with deeper penetration, indicated its tendency to become despotic. Good government according to Aristotle, is that of one, of few, or of many, for the sake of all. A democracy where the many rule for the sake of the many alone, may be a deadly engine of oppression: it may trample without appeal on the rights of minorities and in the name of the common good, establish and enforce an almost unconditional tyranny.'

I suppose an age in which those essential qualities of humanity which belong to working men as much as to all others shall be more prized than the accidents by which one class is separated from another.' We hear much talk to-day about the next age being the age of the Common Man. If this means an age in which the essential qualities of humanity common to the workers as well as to others are more prized than the accidents which separate one class from another, we may welcome its arrival. If it means the stereotyping of the present characteristics of the working class and the domination of society by their particular type, then the prospect is not such a happy one. We have not only to make the world safe for democracy: we have to make democracy safe for the world.

The copy of Maurice's book, *The Representation and Education of the People*, from which the passage protesting against conforming to the will of a majority is taken, belonged to Jesse Collings. His marginal comments are interesting. Of the will of a majority, he says, 'There is no other will on which to base permanent government.' On Maurice's suggestion that the majority might decide for something low and swinish, Jesse Collings observes, 'Poor, egotistical, distrustful of the will, the ideas, the powers of man.' Maurice does indeed express himself as if the majority must always be wrong, but his point is that we cannot identify the will of the majority, the will of the people, with the will of God, and that Bentham's principles give no security that the greatest number will not seek their happiness in low and swinish forms. In this he was certainly right. Utilitarian ethics will not suffice to give moral guidance to democracy. But Maurice was far from distrusting the British people. 'The English people may not be as logical as some others: but they have a certain sense of moral consistency which sometimes supplies the place of logic.' One might also cite his discriminating tribute to the working class in the last chapter of *Representation and Education of the People*. He points out that if the workers were adequately represented,

a whole set of questions which are now most imperfectly handled in the House of Commons—handled by men looking at them from a distance—seeing them from their own point of view—unable to sympathise with the labourers if they wish it ever so much—would then be submitted to fair and reasonable discussion. These representatives of the workers would have no preponderance, but they would have a fair hearing. ...But to attain this blessing, I believe the working classes ought to strive, and that we ought to strive with them for a higher one. They may not only help to adjust claims in which they are themselves interested: they may give a more national, more unselfish tone to the rest of society if only the better thoughts which are struggling in them can be evoked against the lower, debasing, grovelling tendencies which are assuredly struggling in them also. If we consider what kind of effort must have gone to the formation of the co-operative societies, what amount of endurance to the Lancashire distress, what national sympathy to the Volunteer movement, what freedom from the narrowness of John Bullism to the reception of Garibaldi last year—we may understand that there is in this portion of our countrymen something from which we may all derive a wholesome example and a manly impulse. If we remember how much more faith they showed, than any of us showed, in the result of the American struggle, only because they believed it was the struggle of right against wrong, of freedom against slavery: though they had much greater cause than any of us to complain of its effects and to be angry with those who persevered in it; we may feel some humiliation when we assume to be their teachers or prophets.[1]

[1] Pp. 233–4.

Maurice never questioned the need and value of representative government, but he was sceptical about a suffrage based on a property qualification and he was sceptical about manhood suffrage in the sense of universal suffrage, votes for all at twenty-one. In illustrating the first point, I should like to cite a passage which at first may seem rather remote from it, and that is, Maurice's comment on the ejection of Puritan ministers in 1662. Nowadays many novelists and historians who tend to confuse history with romance are hastening to assure us that the Civil War was a struggle between an old order which put moral restraints on commerce and the rising money-power of the bourgeoisie, and that Puritanism was only the religious ideology in which the bourgeoisie disguised their desire for an unrestricted pursuit of wealth. Calvin, according to Mr Belloc, truckled to the bankers and merchants, encouraged them to enrich themselves which they proceeded to do. A Pope, on the other hand, thought that the strength of that heretic was that he cared nothing for money, and for once I think the judgment of the Pope more infallible than the judgment of Mr Belloc. But in any case, our novelists and historians should weigh up this page of Maurice.

The money power now, as then, was threatening to be in the ascendant. . . . But there were some of the circumstances of the time, [the Restoration-period], even of its calamitous circumstances, which tended to check this danger in a class that was most likely to be affected by it. The citizens of the towns had always been in danger of magnifying personal wealth, as the gentry were in danger of magnifying landed wealth. . . . The reverence which they felt for the Nonconformist preachers who resigned their livings [in 1662] was a counter-action to it at this time. The creation of such a body of separatists was, of course, an enormous evil. The persecutions which were inflicted upon them constituted one of the great crimes of the civil and ecclesiastical rulers of Charles's reign. But both one and the other had this attendant blessing—they gave the citizens a set of teachers who had a moral influence over them —a more direct access to their minds than those would have had who used the Prayer-Book. And the sufferings of these men awakened in the trading class a belief in qualities which they would not otherwise have recognised, a respect for the want of the gold which it was the temptation to idolise.[1]

Puritanism never was the simple forerunner of capitalism. Distrusting the money-power, Maurice did not favour a property-qualification for the exercise of the franchise. He wanted manhood-suffrage with tests of manhood. Let a man do something to show that he possessed the spirit of citizenship. Let men show an interest in association, by joining a Co-operative Society or a Trade Union or a Volunteer Corps. Some such qualification would be a proof of manhood and of fitness to vote. Such suggestions will be dismissed as making for a fancy franchise. And Maurice himself realised that we cannot withhold the vote till 'men have demonstrated their fitness for it'. To possess and exercise the vote may be a necessary form of political education. So, in his preface, he wrote, 'We may often doubt whether the exercise of the franchise, *provided the sense of its being a trust could once be awakened*, might not itself be a better discipline, morally and intellectually, for the English citizen than the knowledge, however desirable in itself, which some would demand as the condition precedent to his acquiring it.'[2]

'The sense of discharging a sacred moral obligation.' This leads me to make two further comments on Maurice's

[1] Pp. 127–8.   [2] P. ix.

ethical teaching. He was dissatisfied with utilitarian ethics because its rationalism ignored the sacred character of moral obligation and its individualism underestimated the social character of morality. As Knightbridge Professor at Cambridge, he published two courses of lectures, one on the Conscience, the other on Social Morality. They develop these two points. In the lecture on Conscience, he argues that self-consciousness and moral consciousness, the 'I' and the 'ought', are ultimate and inseparable. His argument is directed against the positions of Bentham and Bain, but it will apply to modern sociologists who see nothing in 'ought' but the authority of society and to the followers of Hume who resolve the 'I' into a string of psycho-physical events. Maurice is very far from asserting the infallibility of the individual conscience, but the individual is none the less aware of a moral law which is part of the order of the Universe. In a preface to the second edition in 1872, which must have been one of his last compositions, he rebutted the criticism of Rabbi Duncan in *Colloquia Peripatetica* to the effect that he, Maurice, cared nothing for law. In the course on Social Morality, which in time precedes the course on Conscience, Maurice urged that while the individual is not just the sum of his various relationships, yet relationships are natural and involve moral obligations and educate us through life itself. Those who, like Robert Owen and one might add like our modern Behaviourists and admirers of Pavlov, stress the importance of external circumstances and external conditioning overlook the essential contribution of relationships. God has set us all in families, and the relation of parent and child enforces the exercise of authority which is not dominion and requires an obedience which is not slavish

subjection. The relation of husband and wife calls for
affection and trust. The meanings of equality and frater-
nity are learned through the normal relations of brothers
and sisters. Maurice includes in the life of the family the
relation of the master and servant which he held to be
inescapable. It teaches respect for service, and the bond
between master and servant is not moralised if it be merely
a cash-nexus.

The school introduces us to a wider circle than the
family. Here we receive our first lessons in citizenship and
find ourselves as members of a particular nation. It is of
God's appointing that the nation binds us by Law,
Language and Loyalty to government. But family and
nation do not exhaust the sources or content of social
morality. It is supremely the function of the Church to
witness to our being members of a universal human
society. The demand for such a society may be discerned
in the communistic settlements of Robert Owen and in
Auguste Comte's cult of humanity. But if humanity is to
become such a society, it must have a Head, a personal
centre. It will depend on a revelation, made not in words
but in acts and in a person. That a Fatherly Will is at the
root of humanity and upholds the Universe is the
announcement which shook the dominion of capricious
demons and the throne of inexorable Fate in the Roman
Empire. To believe in such a Fatherly Will will mean
that we recognise all the good in all men as of God.
It is difficult to believe in such a Fatherly Will unless
God can be touched with the feeling of our infirmities.
Redemption through a God who has suffered with men
is essential Gospel. We must likewise believe in the Spirit
of Truth, in the contemporary inspiration of the Holy
Spirit.

Each main division of the treatise on Social Morality ends with a chapter on Worship, as consecrating the life of the Family, of the nation and of the world-wide human society. Maurice saw in worship the vital link between moral and physical studies, between the humanities and natural science. With his paragraph on this theme this summary of his ethical teaching may fittingly close.

Worship then I conceive becomes the link between Physical and Moral Studies. It vindicates a common ground for both: it asserts Science not Probability to be the aim of both. All restraints upon the freest exercises of human thought by any mortal power it leads us to regard as a defiance of God: all checks upon discovery as indicating an unbelief that He is, or that He is such a Being as Christ has revealed to us. But the severe restraints which Science imposes upon the self-conceit and arrogance which are the enemies of clear free thought, upon the haste which substitutes our judgments and notions for discovery, have their best protection and security in the humility and awe which Worship cultivates, or rather which He to whom the Worship is directed cultivates in us. The moral demands of physical science are, if we may trust its most earnest defenders...quite amazing: we wonder when we think of patience, self-denial, continual surrender of the most cherished notions, which they exhibit and without which they say no progress can be made, no victories achieved. Just so far then as Sacrifice which is the principle and the end of Worship is sought for and obtained, just so far may we look for fresh vigour, for new successes in physical enquiries, because for a deeper and more complete Social Morality.[1]

[1] *Social Morality*, p. 411.

INDEX

INDEX

INDEX